BEYOND OUR DREAMS
Sheila Hawkins

ILLUSTRATIONS
Harry Hawkins

A *Cyprus* **Mail**
BOOK

A *Cyprus* **Mail** Publication

First published in Cyprus in 1997 by
Cyprus Mail Co Ltd
24 Vassiliou Voulgaroctonou
P.O.Box 1144, Nicosia, Cyprus

ISBN 9963-8239-0-4

ACKNOWLEDGEMENTS

My thanks to Harry, the other half of the team, for his brilliant illustrations; to Ian Mair and Graham Parsons for their friendship and formidable computer skills; and to my editor, Steve Myles, for so expertly and unobtrusively cleaning up my act. Finally, a big thank you to Ken Pudney and other steadfast friends who have helped and encouraged me from the beginning.

Sheila Hawkins, Neo Khorio, April 1997

A fishing caique crossed the horizon

v

By the same author

The Back of Beyond

CONTENTS

CONTENTS

DEDICATION

For my brother, David, with love.

MOONLIGHT AND TURTLES

The sea shimmered slick-gold under the setting sun, wavelets flowing like molten metal up over the firm sand. Offshore, gilded whirlpools swirled where restless turtles surfaced, waiting for darkness to fall. Out in the bay a fishing caique crossed the horizon, her tall masts silhouetted against a sky burnished with incandescent red and bronze.

The glorious colours faded and the waterline came alive as ghost crabs *(Ocypode cursor)*, intent on the nightly search for food, began to emerge from their burrows. Weird nocturnal creatures, their prominent eyes standing out on stalks, they vanished in seconds when danger threatened. Scavengers and fierce predators, they were responsible for killing countless turtle hatchlings as they made their way down the beach to the sea.

This was the lovely, quiet time at Lara, a deserted beach on the Akamas coast, where the Department of Fisheries maintained a turtle hatchery to study and protect both the endangered green turtle *(Chelonia mydas)* and the loggerhead *(Caretta caretta)*. With the daytime visitors gone, we were getting on with our appointed tasks; helping to prepare the evening meal, writing up notes, and checking torches and equipment for tagging turtles. The first nest was due to hatch, and from time to time we inspected the cage in the fenced-off area to see whether the hatchlings had come to the surface.

A light appeared out in the bay and a large wooden fishing boat slipped quietly in to anchor in the lee of a low cliff over to our left. The crew were sponge fishers, who had called in earlier and had been invited to dine with us. Their haul of sponges cleaned, they had been out spear fishing - the catch destined for the communal supper.

Washed and changed, the three divers walked along the beach

1

to the hatchery with an assortment of fish suspended on a cord. Giorgos, camp supervisor and superlative cook in *al fresco* conditions, was soon preparing octopus for the charcoal and cutting up selected species for a huge fish soup. The prize specimens, however, were three large *orfos*, the most delicious of fish, to be grilled over charcoal, split open and its succulent white flesh served with olive oil and lemon juice seasoned with herbs.

The boat's skipper, Giorgos (not to be confused with Giorgos, turtle-tracker and chef extraordinaire), had brought me a present. He was a gentle giant of a man, with thickly curling black hair and skin tanned a deep mahogany from years of earning his living from the sea. He smiled, the gold in his teeth gleaming as he handed me a beautiful and unusual sponge shaped like a chalice. It had been cleaned and dried to a pale creamy colour with reddish markings inside.

"These sponges are unusual," he said. "We do not often find them, but this one is for you."

I was delighted with the gift and touched that he should have given it to me when it would have fetched a good price on the tourist market; for sponge fishing was a difficult and sometimes dangerous occupation, carried out by men who were by no means wealthy.

While the fish soup simmered gently, I walked across the still-warm sand to check the nest we were monitoring. There, pressed up against the wire of the cage, was a tiny loggerhead turtle hatchling. The fine sand sifted, and as if by magic another small head appeared, then another, until more than fifty baby turtles were pushing against the wire as they struggled with their miniature flippers to get out, all their instincts driving them inexorably towards the sea.

These hatchlings had a better chance of survival than those from wild nests, for they were protected from predators like foxes, rats, ghost crabs and crows that decimated their numbers as they scrambled to reach the water. We collected them in two or three plastic buckets to take them further down the beach to the point of their release. Later the nest would be dug to ensure none was left floundering at the bottom, and to see whether there were any infertile eggs.

No matter how many times you see a turtle coming ashore to lay, or watch the so vulnerable hatchlings begin their journey to the sea, the miracle of their existence always touches you. You never become blasé about it. Now, everyone came down to where the hatchlings would be released. It was some distance from the waterline, for they needed to imprint the memory of this particular stretch of sand so they would, in time, return to this very beach. The buckets were gently tipped over and the mad scramble for the sea began. One by one the tiny turtles reached the wet sand to be pulled out in the receding waves. Although safe from most land predators because of our presence, some would suddenly stop and start to disappear below ground. One, a few feet away from me, went down in seconds and, with a yell of warning, I dived forward and began frantically digging away the sand from the burrow where I knew a ghost crab was dragging it deep. A sponge diver sprang to help and we reached the turtle, its little flipper held fast by the crab. The crab, so abruptly brought to the surface, released the hatchling at once, intent now only on concealing itself. The baby turtle, none the worse for its close brush with death, battled on to reach the sea. Once there it would face more predators and many dangers, but perhaps this would be one of the lucky few that would make it and return here as a mature turtle to breed.

Dinner was ready, and we sat around the long table to eat and discuss the order of patrolling the beaches later that night. The lamp was turned down low and we spoke quietly, for breeding turtles do not like the distraction of lights and noise. At ten o'clock the sponge

3

divers bade us goodnight and returned to their boat to sleep, while Giorgos, Harry and I set off through an outcrop of rocks to start the first patrol. The moon had not yet risen, but there was enough starlight to enable us to make our way without using torches. We trudged to the far end of the beach, but no tracks showed above the gentle line of surf. Here, we would wait for half an hour. We lay back on the sand, staring at the myriad bright stars that appeared close enough to reach up and touch. This was a time to contemplate the vastness of space and count shooting stars, a phenomenon I never tired of watching and one which was commonplace in July and August. We saw five in that half hour before we started back towards the camp.

Giorgos, with his greater experience, always led the way. He seemed to have the ability to see in the dark like a cat. Suddenly he stopped and put his hand back to warn me and, looking over his shoulder, I saw a fresh track leading up the beach. We immediately dropped down on to the sand and waited while Giorgos edged up beside the track on his stomach. Ten minutes or so went by before he signalled to us with his torch, which had been dimmed so that only a pinhole of light glowed. We crawled slowly and silently up to join him, and I could hear the rhythmic sound of the sand the turtle was throwing behind her as she dug. We waited, silent and unmoving, for Giorgos to check that she had completed her nest and was positioned with her egg depositor over the hole. Intermittently, she sucked in air with a loud, rasping breath. As we inched slowly forwards the moon rose over the cliff at the back of the beach and we could see her clearly. She was a very big green turtle, and already the spherical, leathery eggs were dropping, one by one, into the nest. Now nothing would deter her until she had finished, so we were able to take a closer look and photograph her. Large tears rolled from her eyes as she laboured. As always, when I was so close to one of these

A tiny loggerhead turtle hatchling

beautiful, primaeval creatures, a feeling of awe and wonder swept over me.

She completed her task, and when she had filled in the nest and started to move away, we prepared to tag her. She was big and powerful, single-mindedly intent on returning to the sea as quickly as she could.

"Quick, head her off," said Giorgos, gripping the device that would attach a blue tag to her front flipper.

Easier said than done. She came at me like a bulldozer, shoving me ahead of her, and when Harry caught hold of her right front flipper to enable Giorgos to fix the tag, she almost contemptuously rolled him out of the way and carried on. She was nearing the sea now, and I lay on my back with my feet against her carapace to try and check her. Giorgos rushed to help me, and between us we managed to slow her up enough for Harry, in one deft try, to affix the blue tag. She did not flinch as the tag was attached, nor did she slow her pace. She reached the water and the moonlight reflected momentarily on her gleaming back in the white line of surf. The next instant she was gone.

I wondered where she would travel when the breeding season came to an end. Would someone on a faraway shore see her and contact Cyprus? I wonder still, for although the turtle we tagged with the number forty-seven has returned several times to Lara over the years and has laid many hundreds of eggs, her wanderings in the oceans of the world remain a mystery.

We marked the nest, for in the morning we would transfer the eggs to the hatchery, and returned to base camp for a cup of coffee before Giorgos and I set off in the big land cruiser to check the beach separated from us by the cliffs. As we climbed the steep path leading up to the track where the vehicle was parked, a fox slipped silently through the scrub ahead of us.

"*Alepou*," said Giorgos ruefully.

Foxes are great lovers of turtle eggs, and are very adept at finding them. When they discover and dig a nest they will destroy all the eggs, leaving only chewed and discarded shells as the evidence of their villainy. Once, Giorgos told me, they had been patiently waiting in the dark for a big turtle to finish digging and begin laying. When they eventually switched on the torch it was to see a fox, positioned right behind the turtle, taking the eggs as they fell into the nest.

We drove along the rutted track through fairly dense scrub and low trees until we reached a levelled-out, more open area.

"*Lagos*," said Giorgos, and there, frozen in the headlights, was a large hare.

He doused the lights and it bounded away into the darkness. We saw several more, sitting upright on their powerful hind legs, before we left the car and went down on to the lonely beach. It was a long walk to check this entire stretch of sand, but we were well-rewarded. We did not need torches to see the huge tracks made by the turtles. In the moonlight it looked as though a tractor had been driven up and down the beach. One loggerhead and three green turtles had been up, laid and returned to the sea. We marked the nests carefully. There would be hours of hot work in the morning to dig the eggs and transfer them to the safety of the hatchery.

As we reached the car, we saw a dim light in a clearing. It was Todolos the shepherd, a small, weather-beaten figure with penetrating eyes and a fierce grey moustache.

"*Ella!*" he called.

We went over to his small encampment. His wife had been making cheeses and the two of them were now sitting together, enjoying a simple meal. The shepherdess, with the customary invitation "*kopiaste*", put a fresh *anari* on the table. This cheese, soft when it is fresh and rock hard when it is kept for grating, is cylindrical in shape and bears the markings of the little *talaria* which mould it. She sliced the warm cheese into thick rounds and sprinkled them with a little sugar and *canella*. It was delicious, and although I have eaten fresh *anari* many times since then, it never again tasted the way it did that night, sitting under the stars with the shepherd and his wife.

Time, then, to return to base camp and leave Giorgos to join Harry for a nightcap. I bade them both goodnight and, climbing into the sleeping-bag on my narrow bed, looked up through the rattan shelter at the starlit sky, until the rhythmic pounding of the surf lulled me to sleep.

*****

That night at Lara remains vividly etched in my mind, for it was long before a reasonable road gave access to the remote area and long before the isolated beach fell victim, by day, to the tourist boats, safari jeeps and sun-beds. Then it was a quiet and deserted place, the last major breeding ground in free Cyprus of the green turtle.

By then we had acquired a piece of land on the other side of the Akamas peninsula, and we dreamed of building a house there one day. When friends and colleagues asked where it was we always replied: "It's difficult to describe. It's right out at the back of beyond."

Years later this was to be the title of my first book, and now many people find their way to our door, wanting to see the place for themselves. Almost all ask whether we have had any regrets.

Never. From the first time we stood on the edge of the Akamas wilderness and looked out over the bay, we knew that here we would fulfil our dreams. This was where we would finally put down roots. We had no doubts about the move that would change our lives for ever, but could not foresee that the reality of living in this wild and beautiful place would be beyond our dreams.

MUSHROOM MOUNTAIN

Once his second tour of duty with the Royal Air Force in Cyprus had ended Harry opted for early retirement, and within a year we had settled our affairs in England and returned to the island. We moved into a small rented house in the remote village of Neo Khorio, where we would live while we built our own house further down the valley towards Latchi. We took immediately to village life and began to forge a strong bond with the people. They were friendly and hospitable, and eager to teach us their ways. We learned how their lives were geared to the land and the seasons, and that first year, once the carobs and olives had been harvested, we went with them on the annual trek to Mushroom Mountain.

In November heavy rain had fallen, soaking down into the parched earth, and the beautiful, variegated leaves of the wild cyclamen that flower so profusely in this area were coming through everywhere. In the early morning sunshine following the rain everything looked fresh and invigorated, and the air was filled with the pungent smell of wild herbs.

We had been persuaded to join the regulars from the village going to gather the first *manitaria*. We would not believe how delicious they were, grilled over the fire with a little olive oil and lemon juice and sprinkled with salt and pepper. Moreover, these much sought-after fungi would fetch as much as five pounds an *oke* (a princely sum in those days) in the market if you couldn't manage to eat them all. They were huge mushrooms, but not easy to find if you didn't know where to look.

No problem, we thought. We had long been seasoned mushroom-pickers on various airfields in Lincolnshire and Shropshire. Some we had picked were as big as tea-plates, their creamy-white tops pushing aside the rich soil to show the delicately-pleated undersides. We imagined the appetizing breakfast-smell of bacon and mushrooms sizzling in the pan and we were hooked.

We saddled up Donk (Don Quixote, the donkey we had inherited from RAF Akrotiri) with the big wooden saddle and attached the bags we would bring back stuffed with mushrooms. The only other thing we needed, apparently, was an ordinary kitchen knife each. Sheila the baby donkey, stable-companion to Donk, frisked about, generally getting in the way and making a nuisance of herself. Someone visiting from Akrotiri had brought her up a bright red leather head-collar, and Harry slipped it over her large, velvety ears. She was a pale creamy-beige colour, her baby coat still soft and fluffy, and she looked adorable. Donk, big, strong and dependable, chomped placidly on a carrot while we completed our preparations. Our neighbours were already mounted.

"*Ella, na ba-meh!*" they shouted as they started out. "Come on, let's go!"

Donk stayed dutifully still while I hoisted myself aboard, and off we went up through the village, Harry walking in front leading the donkey foal on a length of rope. Once we had cleared the last house he would let her loose.

Donkey-trekking. It has to be one of the all-time great ways to travel. The early sun was warm on my back as we passed out of the village on to the mud and rock road that led up to the little church of Ayios Minas. No noise of traffic, no irate drivers, no pollution. Donk plodded stolidly on while Sheila, who had walked decorously beside Harry on the lead, now kicked up her heels in delight as she was given her freedom. She galloped madly ahead along the track and out of sight, then came hurtling back, aiming a flying sideways leap at Donk as she passed. Donk snorted, unimpressed. He had seen it all before. He ambled on, pausing now and then to grab

11

Her baby coat still soft and fluffy

12

a mouthful of the new season's grass to munch.

The freshwater spring at Ayios Minas rises among a cluster of pale grey rocks, and Donk stopped to drink from the clear water in the pool. Ptolemos the shepherd had channelled water across the dirt road, and it flowed down into the drinking troughs for his sheep and goats on the other side. The air was full of birdsong, and numerous winter-visiting birds had gathered to drink and bathe.

A muttered (and appropriate) expletive came from Harry as, looking ahead to see where Sheila was, he stepped into a pile of steaming fresh donkey droppings. I swear I didn't laugh. I merely repeated the pearl of wisdom once cast before me by a farmer in our native Devon.

It was when I was assisting the local vet in artificially inseminating an unwilling cow - and she let fly on us in the only manner she could. The rubicund owner of the cow, who was staunchly hanging on to the bad-tempered beast's head while we struggled at the business end, spat noisily and declared with philosophical genius: ``Never 'ee mind m'dear. When us can't smell that, us'll knaw we'm daid.''

Harry was not amused. He wiped his boot in the long grass and ran on ahead, with Sheila galumphing about beside him. Donk and I trudged on, content with our steady pace, until we suddenly met Ptolemos coming towards us with his flock. Donk stopped in the middle of the narrow road and the sheep and goats flowed past on either side of us, anxious to get to the drinking water at the spring. The shepherd halted his donkey alongside mine and we exchanged greetings. He was a big handsome man in his seventies, with a luxuriant white moustache gracing his darkly tanned face. He told me the best places for mushroom hunting and cautioned me to be sure we checked with someone in the village before we ate any. There were *manitaria* out there which might look like the ones we had come to

The shepherd halted his donkey

collect, but which would do us no good at all; and he drew his finger across his throat with a hideous grimace.

We carried on along the track, passing the ruins of what had once been the forerunner of our village. Its name was Paleo Khorio, or Old Village, and it had been built near the spring. A hundred years or so ago, however, one or two families had moved down towards the sea to settle. More had joined them, clearing the pine forest to build their houses and grow crops, and our present village of Neo Khorio, or New Village, was born.

We turned left on to a goat trail that led up through the trees to the mountain. Mushroom pickers were dotted around, shouting to each other across vast distances as they worked. We hitched Donk to a convenient tree, and Sheila, obviously tired from all the rushing about, settled down in the shade near him. We gripped our knives and turned our attention to the *manitaria*.

Half an hour later we hadn't even seen one, let alone collected any. We began to think these giant mushrooms were a bit of a Greek Cypriot myth.

"*Yassoo,* Harry.''

Mushroom George was making his way down the trail towards us, leading an ancient donkey. A small bandy-legged man dressed in faded working clothes, his eyes peered myopically through round, thick-lensed glasses as he greeted us with his usual beaming smile. He drew alongside and we could see that all the bags loaded on his donkey were bulging with mushrooms. They were big all right, but they were not the kind we were familiar with. These fungi, presumably edible, were like orange umbrellas turned inside out, and to us they looked decidedly poisonous. Mushroom George took my knife.

"*Ella na theis,*'' he said. "Come and see.''

Bending down, he brushed aside the fallen pine needles by my

15

feet, and with the knife gently prised up a huge mushroom from underneath a cistus bush. Within minutes he had levered up several more and then watched while we got the idea and started to find them for ourselves. He reiterated the warnings we had already been given about getting someone from the village to check our haul before we ate any.

"These, you see, are very poisonous. Make sure you don't pick any like this." And he dug up an enormous mushroom which, as far as we could see, was absolutely identical to all the others.

Our confidence in finding the right kind of mushrooms somewhat shaken, and our desire to eat them decreasing by the minute, we nevertheless filled our bags before we started back to the village. I got to ride Donk all the way again, Harry preferring to exercise his legs gaming about with the baby donkey. It was late November, and I remember how clear and blue the sky was and how warm the winter sunshine. Tiny wild narcissi *(Narcissus serotinus L.)* were flowering in places, and I dismounted to admire their delicate petals and inhale their fragrance. Donk waited patiently, for he was in no hurry. How I loved this slow pace of life and the way spring appeared to have arrived before summer had even finished.

Further down the trail I could see Harry playing hide and seek with Sheila. She would get very annoyed if, having charged away at great speed, she was unable to find him when she came galloping back. She would bray agitatedly in her funny little baby voice, and when he appeared on the path again, would fall in behind him and push him squarely in the middle of his back with her nose to show her disapproval. Once she had propelled him forward a few times to teach him a lesson, she couldn't resist another gallop down the trail, and off she'd go again.

Thus we progressed as far as the spring at the church, where several mushroom-pickers had already stopped on their way back.

"*Kopiaste!*" they called. "Come and eat!"

Lazarus had a small fire of carob wood burning inside a circle of stones, and he was cooking the first *manitaria* on the end of a pointed stick. Katerina had spread a cloth on a rock, and a plastic plate held the cooked mushrooms over which she had put olive oil, lemon juice and seasoning. Oh well, they had been cut into pieces and everyone was eating from the same plate, so they must be OK. These people had been eating them for years. We washed our knives in the spring water and speared the pieces of mushroom.

The taste was incredible. No wonder they fetched a fiver an *oke;* in London they'd probably have fetched a fiver an ounce in a gourmet restaurant. There was fresh village bread to go with the feast, and pure spring water to drink. Then our mushrooms were tipped out on to the ground, inspected and pronounced good by everyone present. That was a relief - we had a real taste for them now.

On we went down through the village again, where just about everyone came out to peer into the bags and reassure us we had picked the right ones. We were congratulated and fêted as though we had been prospecting for gold and had come back with a bagful of nuggets. We gave some to old Maria, who had no transport and was too infirm to walk very far, and that night we shared our haul with our neighbours, Chrissie and Theodosis, who cooked them over a few pieces of carob wood in the kitchen fireplace. All in all, a memorable day; but, as we enjoyed those mushrooms, we did not know that it would be the first and last time we would pick them.

Before Christmas, Harry developed a violent allergy to something they contain, the toxic effect of which is accumulative. If he eats them again, he may die.

17

The church at Neo Khorio

BEWARE THE KALIKANTZARI

Christmas approached, and the huge overweight porkers we had seen tethered in fields all around the village became restless as every ear-piercing squealing, accompanied by the smell of incense, signalled yet another of their kind being turned into *lounza* and *loukanika.*

The slaughter of the Christmas pig in a village is a ceremonial and important event, although it has long since lost its original meaning of commemorating the killing of all new-born baby boys by order of the Egyptian King Herod. In the not so long ago days before refrigerators were to be found in every home, the smoked, salted or cured meat would feed the family through the winter months up to *Kathara Theftera,* Clean Monday, when, traditionally, all Greek Cypriots go out into the fields and eat only salad vegetables. From then the strictly Orthodox will not eat meat again until Easter, when fat lambs and kids will be slaughtered and cooked in the big outdoor ovens or rotated on spits over charcoal.

Not an occasion for the faint-hearted, the annual pig-killing is an essential part of village life, and we attended a few of these ceremonies. None of them, however, came near the spectacle of the demise of Sophocles' pig, which I described in *The Back of Beyond.*

On Christmas Eve everyone goes to Midnight Mass. The church is packed with people holding lighted candles, and the atmosphere is thick with candle smoke and the smell of incense. After the service people congregate outside the church, shaking hands and embracing and wishing each other *"Kala Christouyenna."*

That first Christmas Eve as we walked slowly down the road to the small house we had rented, we were thinking of our children and feeling sad that they were not with us, but not feeling at all sad

19

to be missing the commercial pressure and hard sell of Christmas in England. Here life was simple, and these friendly hard-working people were, as yet, unspoilt by the tinsel-town mania so prevalent in Europe at that time of year.

We noticed that several people, having returned from the church, were coming out of their houses carrying what appeared to be plates of food. Old Maria was standing outside her little house in the dark, apparently throwing something up on to the roof. She called to us and held out a plate with small pieces of cooked sausage on it.

"This is for the *Kalikantzari*," she said and crossed herself reverently three times.

She told us she was afraid of these grotesque dwarf-like creatures who appeared during the Christmas period. They were either the spirits of babies who had died before they were able to be baptised, or of those poor souls who had no one to sit vigil with them on the night of their death. They were very fond of *loukanika*, she told us, and far better to appease them by throwing some of their favourite food up on to the roof, so they would not come down the chimney and steal the *lounza* and *loukanika* she had hanging on a cord over the fireplace, or dirty her drinking water.

"It is true," she said, "that they are afraid of chameleons. But who can find one now when it is cold and dark?"

No, far better willingly to give them what they want and fix a spray of olive leaves, tied with red thread, to the door. If you have some, you must also sprinkle holy water in every room - to be on the safe side.

She flung a few more pieces of sausage up on to the roof, then held out the plate to us.

"*Ella,*" she said darkly. "You are *xeni in* that house. No

20

Everyone fired up the big outdoor ovens

telling what tricks they might get up to in there.'' And crossing herself three times again, she pulled her black shawl closer around her and hurried inside.

We carried on down the road clutching our *Kalikantzari* offerings and exchanging Christmas greetings with people we passed on the way. We came to a more modern house where a much younger woman was handing bits of food to her two children to throw up on to the roof.

"It's for the *Kalikantzari*,'' she said self-consciously. "Of course we do not believe in them; but they cause a lot of trouble when they are upset, so we do this every year.''

When we got home, it was to find a spray of olive leaves had been nailed to our front door. We looked inquiringly at each other for a moment. Then, together, we threw the pieces of sausage up on to the roof.

*****

The New Year approached and aromatic smoke drifted up from gardens and courtyards as everyone fired up the big outdoor ovens ready to bake the traditional, decorative bread. On New Year's Eve, instead of attending the usual Fancy Dress party in the Mess, we found ourselves crammed into Theodosis' kitchen with his family to celebrate the feast of *Ayios Vassilis.* These celebrations are more important for Greek Cypriots than Christmas, and New Year's Day is when children traditionally open their presents.

Now the festive table groaned under the weight of all the food laid out on it. The centrepiece was the *Vassilopitta,* the New Year cake, in which a coin had been placed before baking. Whoever got the coin in their slice would have great luck in the coming year. This enormous fairly plain-looking cake, with the year '1985' displayed on top in icing sugar, could not be cut until after midnight. Meanwhile, there was a lot of merry-making, eating, drinking and singing to be done. *Kastana* were roasted on the open fire and the levels in the bottles of Anglias brandy got lower and lower. One bottle tipped over, spilling its contents on the floor. Theodosis obviously hadn't chucked enough sausages up on to the roof.

The girls, giggling amongst themselves, gathered around the fireplace to play a New Year's game. They threw olive leaves into the fire, one at a time. Each leaf as it was thrown was accompanied by a traditional chant asking *Ayios Vassilis* to tell them whether their sweetheart loved them. Some leaves just burned, others crackled; but some almost jumped out of the fire with a loud crack, causing shrieks of delight, or much blushing and embarrassment.

Then it was midnight. Time to usher in the New Year and cut the *Vassilopitta.* Chrissie took a large, sharp knife and cut it in four so that the first cut made the sign of the Cross. She then cut it in smaller pieces. The first two slices were set aside, one for the poor and one for the house. Next she served us, as we were their guests. Then everyone, starting with the youngest child, was given a piece. There was a lot of laughter and play-acting as several of the grown-ups pretended to have found the coveted coin before one of the children, who was feverishly throwing cake crumbs in all directions, found it in her slice. Her cousin had been the lucky one the previous year, so all was well.

We wished these warm and hospitable people, who had made us so welcome, "*Chronia polla*" and walked the short distance home, marvelling at the brightness of the stars and feeling optimistic that sometime during the year that had just begun, we would be moving into our own house.

*****

Soon it was Epiphany Day, the celebration of *Ta Phota* - The Light. In the morning the villagers flocked to the church carrying a variety of bottles and plastic containers in which to collect their holy water. *Ta Phota* is the commemoration of Christ's baptism by St. John, and during the service water was blessed in a large copper font. Once the last prayers had been heard the priest donned an apron to protect his robes as, using an old pint beer mug, he ladled water into the receptacles thrust at him from the depths of the rugby scrum surrounding the font. There was great good humour, as well as a lot of pushing and shoving, and then people were streaming along the road bearing the precious liquid which would purify their homes and their livestock. The priest would also visit each house, liberally sprinkling all the rooms and dispelling the last of any evil spirits which may have been lurking around during the twelve days of Christmas.

Later that morning a service was held in Latchi, at which a large silver cross was cast into the sea by one of the local priests. As soon as it was thrown a crowd of young men and boys dived in, hoping to have the honour of retrieving it and handing it back to the priest. Its return, in fact, was never in any doubt, for he had taken the precaution of securing it with a long piece of string before lobbing it in, but it is a well-loved tradition which is repeated throughout the whole of the Greek Orthodox Church every year.

When we returned home one of our neighbours came in with a *kapnistiri* and walked into each room making the sign of the cross through the aromatic smoke. She then produced a pudding basin full of holy water and, with a bunch of olive leaves, shook little showers of water in every conceivable corner of the place before shaking it over us as well.

We felt well and truly purified. The original spray of olive leaves was still nailed to the front door; we had flung some of their favourite food up on the roof to appease the dreaded *Kalikantzari,* and now we had a super-abundance of holy water and holy smoke around the place to ward off the evil eye.

Our own bottle of holy water stood, unused, on the kitchen table. Tomorrow, we decided, we would take it down to the site of our new house - for we had rapidly discovered that the odd gremlin, if not carefully watched, could wreak havoc with the building pro-gramme. Perhaps this would stave off many more occasions when an unrepentant builder, faced with a major disaster, might grin engag-ingly and say "No problem, Mrs Sheila."

WE KNOW HOW TO
CLEAN CHIMNEYS

As it happened, work on our site was progressing well. The concrete floor of the upstairs living-room had been floated in and Yiangos, our builder, now brought some labourers to do the brick-laying.

People from the UK are usually horrified when they see an example of brick-laying in Cyprus. Nothing seems to be in a straight line and everything looks higgledy-piggledy. But here, load-bearing bricks are not used. The bricks are merely to fill in the spaces between the strong reinforced concrete columns which make up the seismic frame; then three coats of plaster are applied, both on the inside and the outside of the building, and the end result is usually a smooth finish inside and an even, rough-cast, white spritz finish on the outside, which looks very attractive topped with a roof of red tiles.

We had earlier encountered one or two problems during the building of the house. The very fact that the foundations had initially been laid so that the house faced completely the wrong way had made us somewhat circumspect regarding our workforce's ability to interpret the plans accurately. We were therefore extremely careful in checking that the gaps for the huge sliding windows were in the right place, and that the gaping hole being left for the fireplace was where we wanted it to be.

Most of the fireplaces we had seen in Cyprus belched smoke in all directions when the wind gusted. You also sometimes got your feet wet sitting by them, as any heavy downpour was likely to come straight down the flue, which was a simple shaft going up through a hole in the roof. Harry decided we were not going to be thus inconvenienced, so he prepared to build the fireplace himself, putting in a smoke-shelf and lining the whole thing with fire-bricks before getting on to the natural stone bit that would grace our living-room.

Petros, a rather rotund figure in shapeless, cement-stained overalls, smiled at the notion.

"*Ochi*, Mr Harry, that is our job," he said firmly.

"But I want to make sure it doesn't smoke..."

"No problem, Mr Harry. When we have finished we will burn a cement bag in it and you will see how the smoke goes straight up."

"But I don't want it straight, I want it like this," said Harry, and proceeded to sketch a plan of the shelf that would stop the smoke being blown back down.

"No problem, Mr Harry," said Petros, taking the piece of paper and putting it in his pocket without looking at it. "We know how to build fireplaces in Cyprus."

Harry glanced desperately at me for help.

"Er, he wants to know if you are quite sure you understand that the hole shouldn't be straight, Petro," I said in Greek.

"Of course. No problem, Mrs Sheila."

There was nothing for it but to leave with good grace. There was a great deal of face to be lost here if we made an issue of it, and we didn't want to offend our workforce.

We went down the rough concrete stairs and Harry carried on with building the stone retaining walls that would comprise part of our garden. A heated conversation started upstairs as Petros and our *mastro,* who had just arrived with a load of wood for the roof, discussed the fireplace. Eventually, the *laspi* came down and started mixing the mortar, which he put in an old metal bucket to be hauled up on a piece of rope.

A reasonable quietness descended as they worked, broken only by shouted demands for more *pilo.* Suddenly there was a loud

27

crash from upstairs. We dashed up and there was Petros, looking at a pile of firebricks which had just collapsed in front of him. When he saw Harry, he immediately began to berate the labourer for the poor quality of his mortar, which had obviously caused the collapse. But never mind, he would soon redo it all.

Harry came down looking gloomy and muttering about the guy not understanding the middle third rule, which meant there was no way he would ever get it to stay up. Sure enough, before lunchtime, another massive crash signalled the second collapse. This time we kept out of the way; perhaps the *mastro* was the one to tell him. Petros was nothing if not a trier, though - he had a third shot at it and called Harry up to inspect the finished work. I came up too, ready to heap praise on his head, and got there just as the impossibly curved construction collapsed in a shower of bricks for the third time.

I thought Petros would be devastated, but he smiled.

"I knew that plan wouldn't work, Mr Harry. It is not the way we do it in Cyprus," and he went cheerfully off to start on something else.

Harry quickly built it the way he wanted, much to the amusement of the team when they saw it. There was no way that queer contraption would ever work. Indeed, we were going to need oxygen masks to be able to sit by it when gale-force winds came across the bay from Turkey in winter. *Kyrie Eleison* - we wouldn't be able to see each other for the smoke.

Their horror intensified when they heard we were going to use huge slabs of natural stone from the Akamas to build and face the fireplace itself, instead of neat rows of bricks which could be painted with cream gloss and have the mortar between them picked out nicely in black.

Before he left that day, Petros fired a parting shot.

"How will you clean the *fugaro* if it is not straight?"

A tingle of alarm swept over me. Harry's past record at

chimney-sweeping was not good. In fact, his last effort marked a bit of a black day in family history.

At the time we had moved into married quarters on an old airfield in eastern England. It was January and bitingly cold, so we lit a fire in the big open fireplace. Harry, never one to be satisfied with a mediocre blaze, soon had a conflagration going that could have roasted an ox. Within minutes, large chunks of soot began to fall down, some of it glowing red. We prudently rolled back the carpet and managed to get the fire out - luckily without setting the chimney alight.

We shivered for a couple of days while we tried to engage the services of a sweep. Not a chance. There was only one locally and he was booked up for weeks. Undaunted, Harry arrived home on day three with a chimney-sweep's set. This consisted of a bundle of bamboo sticks which screwed one into the other, and a flat bristly brush to go on top, all of which fitted neatly into a zipped-up carrying bag. He had everything but the black face, and believe me, that didn't take long.

"Are you sure you know how to do this?" I asked nervously.

"Of course. I've watched the sweep clean my mother's chimney heaps of times - there's nothing to it."

He changed into some old clothes, rolled back the carpet again and covered most of the furniture with sheets of newspaper. Then, kneeling down, he screwed the brush on to one of the poles before pushing it up the chimney. He selected another pole and screwed it into the first, thrusting it further up. He jiggled it and clouds of soot came down to cover everything, including us.

"You'll have to help," he said. "Go out into the garden and tell me when you see the brush come out of the chimney stack."

Glad to be out of there, I pulled on my boots and stood in the snow looking up at the roof. I could hear rattlings and scrapings going on, but no spiky brush appeared. The window was flung open and Harry, who now bore more than a passing likeness to Al Jolson, stuck his head out.

"You're not paying attention. It must be up there by now, I've used up nearly all the rods."

I looked up. There was definitely no brush gracing the top of the chimney. I trudged round to the front garden to view it from the other side, and stood staring in disbelief at the springy poles issuing forth from the chimney and the brush dangling several feet down over the snow-covered roof.

I hesitate to repeat the sweep's remarks, but they were followed with the command that I was not to take my eyes off the brush until it was safely back inside the chimney again.

There was no way I could take my eyes off the damned thing anyway. I was completely mesmerised. After whipping around a bit it eventually disappeared down the chimney and, thankfully, I went indoors to report.

The living-room now resembled the inside of a coal mine, but Harry was clearly discernible by the whites of his eyes.

"OK," he said. "It's plain sailing from here. Just a matter of pull and unscrew, pull and unscrew until the brush comes out."

He pulled and unscrewed, throwing the rods behind him and ducking his head to avoid the showers of soot that came down.

"Pull and unscrew," he chanted as he counted the poles. "Brilliant, that's the last one. This next one's got the brush."

He gave one last yank and the final rod emerged - only it didn't have the brush attached. It was alarmingly bare - the smooth bamboo pole in the grate sported not a single bristle.

It took us days to clean the place properly, and we never did find that brush. But Harry - may Heaven forgive him - looked Petros straight in the eye and said: "No problem, Petro, we know how to clean chimneys in England."

This master of disguises

32

THE VILLAGE OF THE GOATS

The following day we drove up into the wild and rugged country that led towards the abandoned Turkish village of Androlikou. Theodosis had told me that in the old days, the Turks from this village would come daily on their donkeys to Neo Khorio, to sell milk, cheeses and other fresh produce in season. Although the two communities had differing customs and religions, there was no animosity and they lived side by side in peaceful coexistence. Sometimes there had been mixed marriages, and today in our village a Turkish Cypriot man, who is married to a Greek Cypriot, lives and works and is accepted by the whole community. That goes for several other Turkish Cypriots who chose to remain here after the 1974 invasion, when most moved north to live behind the Green Line that separates free Cyprus from the part illegally occupied by the Turks.

Now this formerly Turkish village is deserted, save for the sheep and goats which take shelter in its ruined houses, and the shepherds who tend their flocks. Harry wanted to see how the fireplaces, made from stone found on the Akamas, had been constructed. Here, where most of the houses were in a state of collapse, he was sure he would be able to see just how the old chimney-breasts had been built.

The jeep bumped slowly over the mud track normally used only by donkeys and the odd tractor. The early spring sunshine was warm, and with the hood rolled up around us, the Akamas was ours to savour.

It was springtime and the ground was carpeted with wild anemones, their delicate petals opening towards the sun. Their pink, blue, lilac and violet hues seemed almost luminous among the short grass and spiny burnet, and in one particular area a field of single-colour anemones, massed together, glowed with the deep red of

33

rubies. Wild orchids bloomed profusely, and the air was scented with the overpowering smell of prickly broom, its heavy clusters of pea-shaped flowers making glorious splashes of bright golden-yellow among the green pine and carob trees.

Harry suddenly stopped the jeep and pointed ahead on the road to where a chameleon was making a leisurely crossing. As always here, with time to stop and stare, we watched its wobbling progress as it carefully placed each three-toed foot forward on the ground. It was a nondescript brownish colour, blending in magically with the terrain it was crossing. As it reached a low bank and began to haul itself up among the scrub grass, it gradually changed to pale green, almost disappearing from view as it once again camouflaged itself to fit in with its environment. There was fresh grass growing where water had trickled down the bank, and I couldn't resist picking up this master of disguises and gently placing it among the greenery. It quickly turned bright green and stayed there, motionless, all the time watching us with its protruding, swivelling eyes. I picked it up once more, this time to place it in the cover it sought. It did not hiss at me, as they are sometimes wont to do when threatened, but wound its prehensile tail around my finger and clung tightly to my hand until I held it next to a clump of flowering cistus. Then it carefully reached forward with one of its front legs and gripped a sturdy stem, before releasing each remaining leg in turn to get a good hold on the plant. Only when it had all four feet firmly anchored did it unwind its tail and let go of my finger.

We left it to go about its daily business and drove on, fording a small stream which trickled across the track to disappear among wild oleander bushes and huge rocks lining the sides of a steep ravine. In summer, this stream would dry up completely, but the smooth grey boulders, over which the water now flowed, were evidence of where a once great river had plunged down towards the sea,

There were goats perched on top of stone walls

gouging a deep, narrow chasm in its path.

In one large cavern, between this ravine and another huge gorge where fruit bats populate the remote and inaccessible caves, our former neighbours had made a dwelling place. They were shepherds, and here they lived for most of the year, tending their flock of sheep and goats. The animals were corralled behind fences made from thorn bushes and *Poterium spinosum L.*, the spiny burnet with its matted network of stiff, grey branches, which made an impenetrable mass when piled together. When milking time was over the shepherd would wander with his flock, his characteristic whistling and calling echoing through the clear air as the animals spilled out on to the plateau to feed. His wife remained in the cave, making cheese from the fresh milk and caring for those newborn lambs and kids, too small to graze, that had been left behind with the ewes and goats about to give birth.

The track meandered on through an ancient landscape, little changed over hundreds of years, until it reached the first crumbling stone houses of the old village. There were goats everywhere, goats of all sizes and in an amazing variety of colour combinations. They roamed along the narrow streets, wandering in and out of the empty buildings at will. There were goats perched on top of stone walls, and goats sleeping in the shade of gnarled old olive trees. Half-grown kids leapt and played and chased each other up over steep banks, while a fenced-off garden held captive a dozen or more tiny kids, all bleating plaintively for their mothers.

We parked the jeep in the shade of a huge pine tree outside the old mosque, and pulling on wellington boots, began a tour of the deserted buildings on foot. In one house a large black and white cow lay placidly chewing the cud, and in the garden next door two black pigs rooted and rolled in the mud. An enormous grey and pink sow lay grunting in a straw-filled enclosure while ten or more tiny piglets ran riot, easily able to get out from under the gate which penned in their mother. We practically leapt off the ground when there was a loud crash right behind us and a wooden half-door bulged perilously outwards under the weight of a massive boar which had reared up, and was now poking its head over the top to see what was going on. This was the sire of all the Christmas porkers that met their doom in our village. It didn't look particularly unfriendly, but I fervently hoped the door would withstand the onslaught.

We moved away and turned down another street, glancing in the houses as we went to see if there were any fireplaces in evidence. Some rooms had bales of straw stacked to the roof, others contained sacks of *acheron*. Goat droppings lay thickly over the floors, and a sharp ammoniacal odour pervaded the air.

"This is it," said Harry suddenly. "This is exactly what we are looking for."

He stepped over the threshold of the next house, and taking a deep breath and following him in, I saw that one wall sported a huge stone fireplace. Much of it had fallen down, but the lintel and supporting stones were still in place, and these were the ones he was interested in.

"It's really so simple," said Harry admiringly. "It's made from five big blocks of stone. Two uprights at each side, two on top of those going back into the fireplace, and one horizontal across the top. All I need now is for Andreas to find me the stones and I'll carve them into the shape we want."

Satisfied with the morning's exploration, we retraced our steps and headed for home. Tonight we would go up to the coffee shop and seek out Andreas the Stone.

WHAT'S IN A NAME?

Many English people feel that the entire male population of Cyprus has the name Andreas. This is not true. At least half of them are called Giorgos. Boys are generally named after their fathers and grandfathers, whose ancestors have mainly been given the names of saints or heroes from Greek mythology. As may be imagined, the more important and popular saints have many more namesakes than the others, and this can lead to confusion. The Cypriots do not find it a problem. If a grandfather has the name Constantinos, his son may be Dinos and *his* son Costas. When Costas has a son he may be given the name Costas, but be referred to as Costaki, or `little Costas'. There is always a derivative so that they know exactly to whom they are referring. Not so the likes of foreigners like us. If I mention to Harry in passing that I have seen Andreas, his immediate response is "Andreas who?"

Having, among many others, literally dozens of friends named either Andreas or Giorgos, we needed to come up with a solution to this identity crisis; so we shamelessly stole an idea from the Welsh who, as everyone knows, are all called either Jones or Evans. Jones the Post or Evans the Bread makes the subject of the conversation absolutely clear, so we now have a great variety of labels to go with our erstwhile unidentifiable friends.

To illustrate my meaning and name but a few, we have Mushroom George, Snake George, Orchid George, George the Cement who has the building supply shop, and George the Post, former postmaster of our village.

We have Andreas the Bus, who owns the village transport; Andreas the Turtle who heads the Paphos Fisheries department, Andreas the Sheep who lives in the cave, and the man we now need-

He was short a couple of oxen to do the job

ed to contact, Andreas the Stone.

Andreas the Stone worked up on the Akamas, levering selected slabs of stone from the earth and shaping it for facing and flagging on special building projects. When we went to collect the mail from the coffee shop that evening, Harry told him what he needed and sketched the rough shape and size of each piece on the back of an envelope.

"No problem, Mr Harry," said Andreas, pocketing the drawing.

As always when someone utters these words our hearts sank, for we had learned from experience that this was usually the time to start worrying. Our fears were groundless this time, however, for the following evening he slowed his donkey as he passed the house and told us the stone we wanted was ready.

*****

Early the next morning we set off in our mini-moke to meet up with him. As we passed slowly through the village, the narrow street reverberated to the mighty sound of Theodoulos ploughing his field. Undaunted by the fact that he was short a couple of oxen to do the job, he had hitched two of his donkeys to the wooden ploughshare. Unlike the more placid oxen, which moved, stopped and turned at a simple command, the donkeys tended to do their own thing. Alternatively bawling encouragement and curses at the temperamental beasts, Theodoulos was cajoling and bullying them into dragging the cumbersome plough through the fertile soil. He bellowed his usual greeting as we drove by, and then with a roar that caused a flock of pigeons to rise in alarm, vociferously queried the parentage of his steeds which had suddenly decided to take off while his attention was distracted, yanking him off balance to flounder wildly through the furrowed earth behind them.

We moved hastily on and arrived at the site where Andreas quarried the stone to find him already hard at work. Sure enough, five big blocks of beautiful stone lay ready for loading into the back of the moke. Four of the pieces were big and heavy, but between them, he and Harry managed to load them on board. The fifth block of solid stone, which would form the lintel, was about a metre and a half in length. Although both were strong men, the two of them could not lift it. Fortunately Harry had foreseen this as a likely problem, and had brought along planks and levers. Andreas, with years of experience in moving stone, led the operation while I looked uneasily on, wondering what the Greek for 'hernia' was so I could tell the doctor what had happened.

Unscathed, except for a few bruised and bleeding knuckles here and there, they sat recovering their breath and feeling pleased with themselves, as well they might after all that effort. Then we crawled back along the track towards the village, the sturdy little moke having no problem with its heavy load. Once down at the site, the bricklayers helped push the stones off and get them into a position where Harry could work on them with a pug hammer and claw chisel, to form them into our eventual fireplace.

When he had shaped the blocks of stone, we were faced with the problem of getting them up the rough concrete stairs to the area that would become the living-room. Two men between them could easily manhandle four of the pieces, but the massive lintel was another matter. While we were thinking about it, one of the young and immensely strong building workers, Christakis - who would have been more aptly named Heracles - came down the steps.

"No problem, Mr Harry," he said.

In front of our disbelieving eyes, he picked up the solid block of stone by himself and half ran up the stairs with it. Harry stared, open-mouthed. Even his fellow workers were impressed. I looked at Christakis anew. He was about six feet two or three inches in height, with an athletic build. His smiling face was topped with a mop of tawny-coloured hair and he had a gentle, unassuming disposition. He was, in fact, rather shy. His hands were huge, dwarfing most other men's when they shook hands. He spoke virtually no English, but was a willing and industrious worker, laying at least twice as many bricks in a day as the others. The phenomenal strength he so took for granted became evident on many more occasions. One I particularly remember was when we had run out of cement. I was detailed to go in to Giorgos the Cement to replenish our stocks, but in order that work should not be held up while I was away, Nathanielis, the *mastro* who was building a house on the opposite side of the valley for Alfons and Helli, our only neighbours, offered some of his to keep us going. Christakis went across the dirt track and up three flights of concrete steps to where the bags of cement were piled, and once again he astonished us. He *ran* down the steps, across the lane and up our flight of garden steps with one bag of cement under his arm and another balanced on his shoulder. The combined weight of two bags of cement is about 100 kilos, and most average men would find it difficult to lift just one and carry it all that way without a bit of a struggle.

With Christakis' help the huge lintel was positioned correctly, and today the roughly-hewn fireplace, with its traditional shape, faced with natural stone from the Akamas in subtle terracotta shades, still stands firm. Not only does it keep us warm and provide a focal point to sit around and toast pieces of *halloumi* and *lounza* on winter evenings, but, with a *serpentina* of copper pipes which Harry plumbed into the solar heater, the blazing log fire provides us with all the hot water we need. And it doesn't smoke either!

BATHROOM DISASTERS

We seemed to spend quite a lot of our time recovering situations handed on to us by various well-meaning builders, some of whose problem-solving ideas left something to be desired.

Alfons had just been at the mercy of an electrician who came to install a heating system in a small extra bathroom next to the master bedroom. All seemed to go well inside the bathroom and he watched approvingly while the workman placed the switch on the wall outside in the narrow hallway. He tried the heater and it worked! He could hardly believe his luck - there was not much mess, and the installation had only taken a couple of hours. When winter came and there was very little heat from the solar heater, he would have instant hot water at the touch of a switch.

Alfons swept up the dust in the hall and closed the bedroom door. He turned and noticed that the bathroom heater was on. Puzzled, he switched it off. A few minutes later, Helli opened the bedroom door and the heater turned itself on again. They quickly realised that the switch had not been set flush with the wall, but protruded just enough so that every time the bedroom door was opened or closed it pushed the switch into the 'on' position.

After several days of being driven mad by the switch clicking on and off he managed to contact the electrician.

"No problem," said the workman, having already been paid for his efforts. "Leave the door open."

Alfons insisted that the matter be rectified.

"*Avrio,*" said the obliging man.

A few *avrios* and telephone calls later he eventually turned up, carrying not a screwdriver with which to remove the switch, but a small saw. Alfons immediately sensed that something was amiss and watched his every move, intervening in the nick of time as the imperturbable workman prepared to cut a wedge out of the side of the beautifully carved bedroom door.

The situation was finally properly resolved, but it was another reason for us to be wary of letting anyone loose, unsupervised, when it came to technical work or getting a good finish. Thus when we were ready to build our bathroom, local plumbing being a bit of a hit and miss affair, Harry decided he would do it all by himself.

We had purchased a beautiful bathroom suite in a warm beige colour, and I had managed to find plain toning wall tiles which, here and there, had four placed together to form an attractive group of trees in the exact colour of the porcelain.

Harry acquired a pipe-wrench and other tortuous-sounding equipment with which to install our beautiful bathroom, and having done all the essential plumbing, he made sure it worked and photographed it for future reference. He then got Christakis to assist him in lifting the bath into position. We were delighted with the way it looked and, with the ceiling finished, it was time to cover the walls from top to bottom with our Italian designer wall tiles.

"I hate tiling," said Harry. "I'd rather do the plumbing bit any day."

"OK," I said. "Let's get someone to do it for you. It's a fairly straightforward job. Leave it to me - I'll find someone who knows what they are doing."

Those words came back to haunt me later, but always being an optimist, I found an engaging chap who assured me that he and his brother, who was a building *mastro* somewhere in Nicosia, had tiled hundreds of modern bathrooms before. He would come and do the job on Thursday.

"I have to go to Limassol on Thursday," said Harry. "You

44

can keep an eye on him, can't you?''

My new workman arrived on time and was soon hard at work in the small bathroom. Every time I made him a cup of coffee or asked if he was OK, I got the reply I was only too familiar with: "No problem, Mrs Sheila." So I left him to it.

Shortly before he was due to finish work in the afternoon he came upstairs and stood looking, I thought, somewhat uncomfortable. I smiled at him inquiringly.

"*Birazi,* Mrs Sheila?'' he said.

Alarm bells started clanging in my head. Does what matter? I hardly dared find out. I followed him down to the bathroom where he stood staring forlornly at his day's work.

"I think it might *birazi* a bit when Mr Harry sees it,'' I said slowly.

By now he was looking thoroughly miserable and I could hear our vehicle coming up the track.

"*Then birazi,*'' I heard myself saying - "it doesn't matter.

You go on home now and I'll sort it out with Mr Harry.''

His face lit up and he was on his motor scooter and away down the lane before Harry had climbed out of the jeep.

His day in Limassol had gone well. Now he was glad to be back and eager to inspect and admire our newly-tiled bathroom.

"Has he finished?''

"Yes, but...''

Harry immediately sensed a disaster.

"Oh no. Don't tell me he's put the trees in the wrong place.''

"Er, no, but...''

"Oh God, he's put them upside down, hasn't he?''

"Er, no...''

"Well, he said he'd done wall tiling before, didn't he? So

there's not much else he can have made a pig's ear of in there.''

Really?

"Well go on, tell me what happened.''

"He wants to know if this *birazis.*''

Harry stepped past me into the bathroom and stood there staring in disbelief at our lovely tiles sliding askew on a mountain of wet grey plaster, which was several inches thick near the ceiling and almost non-existent near the floor. In places the valiant workman had tried to reduce the amount of plaster he was building up and, in so doing, had given the wall some interesting curves.

As we gazed at the unusual configuration, one of the topmost tiles fell off and Harry's hand automatically shot out to catch it.

"He says the walls weren't straight,'' I ventured.

"They sure as hell aren't now.''

Then, resignedly, he pulled off his shirt.

"Come on, we've got to get them off and scrub them clean before it all sets like concrete on us.''

I deftly fielded another tile as it slid off the wall and we began, not for the first time, the back-breaking, soul-destroying, time-consuming task of demolition - to be followed, hopefully, by recovery.

Looking back, though, on a bathroom disaster scale of one to ten, I have to admit it didn't come near Bill Watson's toilet.

*****

Bill and his lovely wife Mary are good friends of ours. They live on the other side of the mountain in a small village on the southwest coast. Their house is full of traditional charm and has a delightful enclosed garden. There, sitting under the sun umbrellas, lunch can take up to two or three hours while we converse over a bottle of chilled white wine.

The first time we visited them I asked if I might wash my hands before lunch, and was directed to the bathroom. When I returned to the table I congratulated Bill on his innovation in having a sunken bath put in.

"Ah," he replied thoughtfully. "I'm glad you like it. To tell you the truth, though, it wasn't exactly what I had in mind when we started."

He told me that when they began renovating the old stone-built house, one of their main priorities was the installation of a modern bathroom. They wanted it simple but functional, with hot and cold running water, a bath, a washbasin and a toilet. They ordered the porcelain suite, then scoured the area for a suitable workman who knew something about modern-day plumbing.

They found just the man, who came highly recommended by everyone in the village. (Easy to remember, with hindsight, that hardly anyone else in the village at that time even had a toilet, other than the earthen dropping zone in the garden over which was positioned a chair with no seat.) So, with impeccable references, their chosen man came to look at his task.

Firstly, said Bill, a floor would have to be laid, which he would like surfaced with marble tiles, please.

"No problem," said the expert. "I will make you a bathroom to be proud of."

His troubles over, Bill took his wife to England on holiday while the disruptive work was in progress.

When they returned they were, of course, anxious to inspect their new bathroom. They couldn't wait to open the door. When they did, it was to stand there in utter amazement staring at the sunken bath, a washbasin only Quasimodo could have used, and a toilet, its lid neatly closed, the seat of which stood just a couple of inches above the ground.

It appeared that, when the intrepid workman had finished the plumbing, he decided to carry on and install the bathroom suite *before* he laid the floor. This, as it turned out, was not a good idea - because he forgot to make allowance for the sand, mortar and marble tiles which would considerably raise the finished level of the floor above the height he had started with.

"It was terrible on the knees," said Bill. "I wouldn't have minded, but we weren't getting any younger and, once we got down there, we couldn't get up again."

With great difficulty, and a lot more mess, the washbasin and toilet were raised to an acceptable level, but there was no way the penitent builder was going to move that bath. So there it remains today, a sunken monument to the genius of the Cypriot workman and a warning to all other optimists.

I still think it's a great idea, and I wish we had one...

THE GOLDEN CITY

Once we had moved into our new house, I found myself more and more drawn to the beauty of the bay of Chrysochous. The land below the house drops gently away, the slopes clad in evergreen scrub with scattered carob, pine and olive trees. From here we look down on the little fishing port of Latchi, slowly growing now into a modern tourist resort but, thankfully, lacking in tall and unsightly apartment blocks. Most of the area is still undeveloped, and buildings more than two storeys in height are not permitted. The bay curves around eastward to a wooded promontory which houses the Polis camping site, then sweeps on, passing several small villages, until it reaches the point at Pomos. Behind the azure waters of the bay the land rises up again, to form the lovely backdrop of mountains which feed water to the fertile plain below and provide shelter from cold easterly winds in winter.

Chrysso in Greek means 'gold', and there are differing theories as to why the area was given the name Chrysochous. Gold and silver were mined here as far back as the time of the Venetians, and I tend to support the view that this was the main reason; for it was then that Polis tis Chrysochous was given its name. The mines are at Limni on the opposite shore of the bay from our house, and another precious metal, copper, was also mined here. Evidence of copper-mining and smelting in Cyprus dates back to 1000 BC. The very name Cyprus is derived from the Latin word *coupros,* meaning copper, and at one time this island was the main supplier of copper to the Roman Empire. There are old Roman workings at Limni, where the miners worked along galleries shored up with wood and brought out the ore in locally woven baskets.

Limni is the Greek word for 'lake', and the place was given

A doorway in the golden city

its name from the lakes that formed in craters left when the ore was extracted. A wooden jetty, dating from fairly recent times, stretches out into the sea, and here, in the early part of this century, the copper was loaded on to boats for transportation to foreign shores. When the ore was washed, the sea turned a golden-yellow colour. Some believe 'the bay of gold' derives its name from this. Others subscribe to the name having been given to the area because of the richness of its fertile soil.

Whatever the reason, Polis tis Chrysochous, the golden city, is well-deserving of its name. For this small town stands on the site of the two great former kingdoms of Marion and Arsinoe. After the Trojan war the city of Marion was built by the Athenian Akamanthus and destroyed in 312 BC by one of the Ptolemies of Egypt. Another Ptolemy, Philathelfos, later rebuilt it and named it Arsinoe after one of the female members of his family. A wealth of riches and precious artefacts has been discovered in the town over the years, and one or two construction sites have had development halted by the government, as the digging of foundations for new buildings has revealed ancient dwellings or part of the old city walls beneath. Most local builders have stories of finds unearthed - large earthenware jars filled with silver Ptolemaic coins, decorated pottery dating far back into history, and gold jewellery, much of it in delicate filigree work set with turquoises, from the Byzantine period.

Modern day Polis is lucky to have an administration proud of its ancient past and keen to preserve its Cypriot culture. The central square is one example of how the town has, in the main, retained its traditional character and not become a faceless chrome and glass facade like so many other places before it.

Apart from the long-closed mines at Limni, the Polis area has traditionally been one of farming and fishing. The lovely climate and

A wooden jetty stretches out into the sea

rich soil allow year-round production of fruit and vegetables, and although the Troodos mountain regions have magnificent crops of apples, pears, cherries and plums, the warmer coastal plain produces oranges, lemons, grapefruit and bananas, nectarines, peaches, loquats and apricots, while melons and avocados ripen alongside fields of tomatoes, cucumbers, peppers and courgettes.

The new growth industry of the region, however, is tourism. Here we have it all. Breathtaking scenery, a beautiful climate, warm unpolluted sea and hospitable people. There are sandy beaches and sheltered inlets; and mountain roads which lead up into the forest, past tranquil dams where wild *moufflon* seek water and Imperial eagles soar. On up through a landscape that can only be described as majestic, with its towering pines and steep escarpments, until past the Forestry Station at Stavros-tis-Psokas, the road leads on to the incredibly beautiful Cedar Valley, where drifts of tall blue cedars entwine their fragrant branches under a cloudless sky.

The Paphos forest is a delight. In spring wild flowers abound and the pure song of the nightingale echoes through the trees. In the summer months you can seek welcome shade and walk the nature trails laid down by the Forestry Department. Here, on a clear day from the highest point, you can see the snow-capped mountains of Turkey. And the air you breathe is like wine.

Then, of course, there is the Akamas to explore, an unspoilt expanse of forest, caves and mountain tracks which lead always to the jewelled sea. It was here that Aphrodite came to bathe in deep seclusion with her handmaidens. Wild and rugged, it has suffered earthquake, fire, drought and foreign raiders. Earlier men have come and gone, and sometimes left their mark, but still it has endured. Long may the ancient Gods protect it.

HIDDEN WONDERS

The Akamas wilderness is a mysterious area of which little is known. It contains many tombs and burial chambers from earlier civilisations, and one hundred and one churches are recorded as having been built on the peninsula. All have been located save one, and the whereabouts of this still remain a mystery. The sites of these former old churches and monasteries are revered by the village women, who take candles and oil and pray there, as their mothers and grandmothers did before them. Some churches, as in the case of Ayia Zoni in an almond grove just a few hundred metres from our house, have only part of a huge stone column left to show where people once gathered to worship.

The whole area is riddled with caves. It is mainly made up of limestone laid down over the millennia by living sea-creatures. Even on the highest points of the Akamas you can find pieces of sea coral and the fossilised remains of other marine life which thrived in the waters of thousands of years ago.

The porous rock holds moisture like a sponge, and the flow of water, continually wearing away at the rock and dissolving out minerals, has created labyrinths of caves, many of which have yielded up evidence of early man.

But still this remote area remains a mystery, its secrets as yet undiscovered. Is there really a lost city of Akamas, and does it now lie somewhere beneath the sea? Will someone, some day, uncover by chance a clue that will give a brief glimpse into an earlier age, and will this lead to an astounding archaeological find? There are always those who, full of daring and filled with the desire to be the first to go where no modern man has gone before, will investigate every rumour and follow every lead in search of a key to unlock the door to the past.

Two such young men live here, and on a cold and windy January day with waves pounding against the harbour wall at Latchi, I went down to the diving and water-sport centre to hear, at first hand, the truth about a remarkable cave they had discovered and explored a few months earlier. This is their story.

*****

Tall and athletic with sun-bleached hair pulled back from his tanned face, Hans, originally from the Netherlands, has been running the dive centre for many years. Minas, the youngest son of the Tappas family of divers from Neo Khorio, works there with him. When we first came to the village Minas was a beautiful boy with huge dark eyes and a lovely smile. Now he has grown into a handsome young man, and with his knowledge and experience of boats, is a great asset to the centre. Both men are adventurous and ever keen to participate in new discoveries in the region where they live. Hans in particular is always on the lookout for caves to explore, and when Minas one day mentioned that his father knew where there was a deep hole in the Akamas above the village, his interest was instantly aroused.

However there was one obstacle to overcome. Minas' father, Mikhalis, would not tell them where it was. It was an evil place, and no villager would go near it. Some said it was the haunt of the devil, while others believed a fire-breathing dragon lived there, for at times smoke could be seen issuing from the ground.

This only served to whet their appetites, and the more Mikhalis told them, the more Hans and Minas wanted to see it for themselves. Mikhalis, already having suffered the tragic loss of two of his sons, was reluctant to point the dare-devil fearless Minas in the direction of a place that, to him, seemed fraught with danger. They pestered him for months, but still he held out. Then, unexpectedly, he changed his mind. When summer came, deciding he could take no more of their constant badgering, he gave in. He would lead them to the hole.

On a lovely, warm, sunny day they set off towards the Akamas, and abandoning the vehicle when the track finally became impenetrable, they proceeded on foot into the forest. Mikhalis could remember roughly the area but not the exact location of the hole, so they split up to broaden the base of their search through the trees and scrub.

"Here it is!"

Hans' voice was charged with suppressed excitement. The three of them stood looking at an opening, measuring about a metre across, in the floor of the forest. Hans shone a torch down into the black void. They could see nothing. He dropped a stone into the centre of the hole and listened intently. They heard nothing. Mikhalis was uneasy, and the initial electrifying enthusiasm felt by Minas had worn off. When Hans suggested they go down inside to explore, Minas, the fearless dare-devil, took one look into the hidden depths and unequivocally replied.

"No way."

Hans, an experienced caver, donned a safety helmet to which he attached a powerful lamp, and securing a rope on the surface, dropped it down into the black hole. He adjusted his harness, and pumped up with adrenalin, let himself over the edge and abseiled down into the pitch blackness below.

After a few metres the walls widened out and he found himself in an enormous cavern. At once he was bedazzled and overcome

Through rows of giant stalactites

with awe as the powerful beam of his head-lamp revealed he was travelling down through rows of giant stalactites, forming huge columns which gleamed like white marble. As he turned his head to gaze in wonder at this phenomenon, he saw others cascading over the walls of the cave, the deposits glistening in the beam of his light with pastel hues of rose-pink, ivory, blue, green and white.

Hans shook his head at the recollection of that first descent. It was, he said, like going down through a huge vaulted cathedral. He could hardly believe his eyes. Stalactites had not previously been found in Cyprus, and here, suddenly, were these massive formations in an incredible array of glorious colours.

The magnitude and magnificence of the place in which he found himself threatened to overwhelm him. He began to lose touch with reality and almost became disorientated, but the discipline and skills he had acquired over the years as a diver now came to the fore; he turned his attention to the descent, determined to reach the floor of the cave.

At last his feet touched the bottom, and immediately he sank up to his knees in something that felt like fresh snow. The floor was made up of layer upon layer of bat droppings, almost a metre thick, on top of which grew a strange green fungus. The heat generated from this as it decomposed, Hans realised, was the source of the devilish smoke the villagers saw issuing from the hole. Leading away, and down, from the cave itself was a narrow tunnel. He made his way towards it, eager to see where it led.

He reached the entrance and looked back to see his footprints etched deeply in the soft surface like tracks across a snowfield. It made him acutely aware that he was the first man to have walked here in many hundreds of years. At once elated, yet humbled, he ducked his head and entered the tunnel.

It was long and narrow, and sloped fairly steeply downwards.

58

In places he could almost stand upright, but in others he had to crawl on hands and knees. When he had progressed some little way inside, his euphoria abruptly vanished and a cold dose of reality struck him. What if his lamp went out? He had only the one on his helmet. What if he became stuck, injured or lost? Far above him, his two companions, with whom he had now lost contact, would not come down into what they perceived to be a hell-hole. He hesitated, torn between the compelling desire to carry on with his exploration and the knowledge that it would be foolhardy to do so alone in these unknown circumstances. Common sense prevailed, and reluctantly Hans retraced his steps across the floor of the cave and started the long climb up, through the superlative splendour of the gigantic stalactites, to the surface.

As he ascended he could hear the faint voices of Mikhalis and Minas as they called anxiously down to him. He shouted back that he was on his way up, and soon willing hands were helping him through the hole.

At first he could not find words adequate to describe what he had seen - his native tongue was Dutch and their language, of course, was Greek. But, conversing in English, he managed to convey to them the marvels he had seen and the fact that there was a tunnel which, he suspected, must lead to another cave. Minas' spirit of adventure quickly overcame his instinctive fear of the legendary black hole, and soon he was buckling on the safety-harness and abseiling down into the glistening, pastel-tinted world of stalactites.

When he too surfaced, full of the wonders of the place, there was nothing for it but for Mikhalis to go down as well and, like them, be all but overwhelmed by the spectacle he encountered below.

They returned to Latchi for more equipment. On reflection, Hans was more than ever convinced that the tunnel he had started to explore led into another cave, and that too would probably have an opening to the surface.

Back in the forest, with one or two friends to help search and assist in any rescue that might be necessary, they systematically covered the area in the vicinity of the original hole, looking for an entrance to the cave Hans felt convinced was there. He was shortly to be proved correct.

A voice echoed through the forest.

"I've found it!"

Sure enough, a little more than a hundred metres from the first hole was a second. This time there was no holding Minas. Quickly scrambling into the climbing gear, he dropped down through the opening and was lost from sight. Almost at once they heard his voice, charged with excitement, calling up to them.

"There are pots here in the walls!"

He shouted the same thing several times then, at one point:

"*Panayia mou!* There's a skeleton here."

He was crawling along a tunnel which soon widened and went vertically down for approximately six metres, before opening out into two medium-sized caves - one on either side of him. The one to his left came to a dead end. Retracing his route, he entered the other cave. He made his way to the bottom and saw that there was a hole situated centrally in the floor. By now he was about fourteen metres under the ground, and shouting up that he was going on down through a further tunnel, he climbed over the edge and continued his careful descent. This narrow connecting tunnel went vertically down for a few metres and then suddenly opened out into a huge cavern almost three times the size of the Aladdin's cave of stalactites they had just discovered.

The distance from here to the lowest point of this colossal cavern was fifty metres, and the floor was littered with amphorae.

60

More amphorae lay in cul-de-sac passageways leading off to one side. Then came the realisation that Hans' theory had been correct, for the floor sloped upwards, and where it met the side wall, a tunnel led off. It was the one Hans had started along from the other cave. When Minas finally reached the end and shone his light inside, Hans' footprints were clearly defined in the strange, soft surface of bat droppings and fungi.

Having crouched and crawled his way through the connecting tunnel, Minas stood upright in the first cave, gazing spell-bound at the columned formations of glistening stalactites, against which were cast eerie winged shadows as sleeping bats became disturbed and fluttered across the beam of his torch.

When they had completed their explorations that day and returned to the surface, they were only too well aware of the extreme importance and uniqueness of their discovery. They left everything the way it was and returned to base, where they reported their amazing find to the authorities.

A few days later a government team arrived, bringing various experts to examine the whole cave system. They reported that it was not a burial site, that the stalactites were the first ever recorded here, and that tools and amphorae found in the caves dated back to the very early Bronze Age. In fact they were the earliest ever Bronze Age artefacts to be discovered in Cyprus.

The government's decision was to seal off access to the caves and not make public their location. Perhaps some future archaeologists may, one day, find themselves with sufficient funds and equipment to investigate this ancient site properly.

Meanwhile, somewhere below the leaf mould and pine needles that cover the forest floor in the untamed Akamas, lies a wondrous cavern adorned with giant columns of pearly stalactites, their lustrous sheen and delicate colours unappreciated by the unseeing bats that inhabit the upper regions of the cave.

A LASTING MEMORIAL

As well as caves there are several uninhabited derelict villages on the Akamas, and not so very far from our own village, magnesia used in the making of crockery was mined. In the old colonial days the mines were owned and operated by the British, who took out the best quality ore, leaving behind a large quantity of second grade material. The local people later took over the mining operation, building circular kilns near the sunken shafts to extract the pure mineral. The magnesia was loaded up on to camels owned by a Turk from Yiolou, an old Turkish village several miles behind Neo Khorio, and taken over the mountain along an established camel trail which led down to the shore near the Baths of Aphrodite. Here a sturdy wooden pier jutted out into the sea, and the cargo was loaded on to large ships which came regularly from Czechoslovakia. Some of the older men still living here today used to work in the mines, plying to and from the village by donkey. Now the deserted mines lay hidden under the sun-baked earth, and only the bats, hanging silently from the ceiling in the deep, dark recesses of the man-made caverns, sense the ghosts of long-dead miners and hear the phantom cries of the old Turkish camel driver from Yiolou.

From the forgotten mines the camel trail winds up over the mountain and down through rugged and spectacular scenery towards the coast. The Forestry Department has mapped out and marked nature trails in the area, and visitors can now walk along part of the trade route once used by the camels. One trail ends near the legendary Baths of Aphrodite, a secluded grotto where the Goddess used to bathe in a pool of clear water fed by a spring trickling down over the rock face. It is an area of great natural beauty where the wild cyclamen, for which the Akamas is famed, bloom profusely in the early spring. The water finds its way to the sea via a lush green

Circular kilns near the sunken shafts

gorge clad in trees and shrubs which nightly release the fragrant scent of herbs, so evocative of this lovely island, into the warm air; and when the moon rises over the bay and bathes the scene in its pure light, it is easy to feel the mysticism that drew the ancient worshippers of Aphrodite to this place.

A tourist pavilion stands on the edge of the cliff, and here you can sit and absorb the glorious view, or walk down the long flight of steps to the pebbled beach and swim in the warm sea. This coast has no shipping lanes and very little development, so the water has an amazing clarity, changing in colour through various shades of turquoise, green and peacock blue as it passes over the different surfaces beneath. Brightly coloured stones show clearly through the crystal water, and the sheltered inlet is surrounded by rocks where migrating herons and egrets rest during their autumn migration.

One rock, now a famous landmark, stands alone with a white cross on top. The rock itself, rising up out of the water in this lovely setting, is extremely beautiful - coloured pink and green by its mineral content - and the sea around it seems to take on the deep, mysterious hues of malachite and lapis lazuli. Tourists, stopping to admire and photograph it, are always curious about the origin of the cross, so if you ever visit this picturesque area, spare a thought for the young soldier who died so tragically here far away from his home.

He was one of the United Nations peace-keeping contingent formerly stationed in Polis Chrysochous, and his great passion was for diving and snorkelling in the warm waters of the Mediterranean.

One of the local fishermen, who also dived for sponges, was a special friend of his. Loukas Karamanas still lives and works here, and to research the story of the boy's tragic death, I went to find him at his restaurant, The Lemon Garden in Polis. I have known Loukas for some years; he is a tall, good-looking man with a ready smile, but an expression of sadness came over his face when he recalled the event. This is what he told me.

Next to his house he has a shop which supplies fishing tackle, diving gear and the like; and the young foreign soldiers, interested in fishing and diving, soon came to know him well. He recounted tales of the many impromptu parties which took place at his restaurant when one of them came back with a good catch and he cooked it for everyone to enjoy.

He and this particular boy used to go diving regularly - sometimes with a compressor, but more often just with a snorkel mask and harpoon-gun. A previous evening the two had been snorkelling together but, on the night of the tragedy, for some reason the young soldier decided to go on his own.

When he did not return to barracks the alarm was raised, and his friends contacted Loukas and asked for his help. He immediately went out with his boat and searched along the coast where they normally fished. When dawn broke and he had scoured every inch of the shallow bays and inlets repeatedly with no success, he returned to the harbour and telephoned the British base at Akrotiri for assistance.

The Royal Air Force's response, as always in an emergency where lives are at risk, was immediate. A helicopter from 84 Squadron was scrambled and quickly arrived on the scene. The bright yellow aircraft hovered above the rock and, from their high vantage point, the crew looked down through the crystalline depths. They saw the boy, seemingly held fast near the bottom in several metres of water. When they sent divers down to recover the body it quickly became evident what had happened.

Equipped with snorkel mask and harpoon-gun, he had gone fishing alone near the Baths of Aphrodite. He successfully speared a very big grouper, but then made the mistake of tying it to his belt

A lasting memorial

66

before swimming down after another large fish. He had the second one impaled on his harpoon when the huge fish, which he had tied to his waist and had wrongly assumed to be dead, fled into a cleft amongst the rocks and became wedged, effectively anchoring him to the sea-bed. No knife was found on his body.

Some time later his comrades erected the white cross on the rock above the place where he had lost his life. It stands there to this day, a lasting memorial to a young soldier in a place of outstanding beauty.

CHURCHES OF BYZANTIUM

Cyprus is never more beautiful than in spring, when the countryside is bedecked with flowers and blossom, and the warm scented air drones with the murmuring of honey bees. Birds are resplendent in their mating plumage, some, like hoopoes, golden orioles, rollers and bee eaters providing exotic splashes of colour in and around the garden.

One April morning, not for the first time, a wryneck woodpecker landed, exhausted, on the kitchen window-sill. It has appeared regularly on migration year after year, staying for a day to feed well in the garden before moving on. It is an unusual bird with beautiful barring across its plumage, and I looked at it closely again, lost in admiration. Its scientific name is *Jynx torquilla,* and in Greek mythology it is associated with the witch Iynx.

Iynx was the daughter of the nymph Echo and the Arcadian god Pan. She was foolish enough to use her witchcraft to cast an erotic spell on Zeus, and his jealous wife Hera turned her into a wryneck.

In ancient times the bird was used in binding magic and its use as an erotic charm is recalled today in the word `jinx'. It released me from its spell and flew silently away to cast a jinx on someone else. I was sorry to see it go, but glad that, for some reason, it chooses to rest awhile with us each year on its long journey.

*****

With the advent of spring Harry was keen to continue our

Checking that all was well with his harem

exploration of the countryside. He had heard of two or three old Byzantine churches in the area which, although not in general use, had not fallen into ruins and he was itching to find, photograph, and draw them.

We decided to set aside a day before the weather began to get too hot, and devote our time to exploring the territory further inland and seeking out these lovely old buildings.

Armed with sketch-pad, cameras, a flask of coffee and a picnic lunch, we drove the jeep towards Polis and off the beaten track, following the crudely-drawn instructions we had been given by various people who professed to know where to find the churches.

It was a lovely warm day, and the sun shone down from a cloudless sky. The grass was still lush and green after the winter rains, and the unploughed fields were full of golden-yellow daisies and scarlet poppies. Donkeys turned their heads to watch us pass, swishing their tails and blowing hard down their nostrils, before getting back to the serious business of munching their way through the plentiful greenery. In several meadows tiny foals gambolled around tethered mares, almost lost from sight in the luxuriant growth of long grass and flowers.

We turned off the small road on to a practically non-existent track and soon had to stop - finding ourselves in the midst of a sea of sheep. There were two hundred or more, and they jostled and pushed their way around us. One large ram, with a bell attached to a leather collar round its neck, looked anxiously around checking that all was in order with his harem while the ewes bleated plaintively to keep in contact with their lambs.

The shepherd, leaning on his stick, greeted us warily; he was not used to seeing strangers in this isolated place. His weathered face broke into a mainly toothless grin when I answered him in Greek, and there followed the usual enquiries as to our success at procreation and profuse congratulations on having produced a girl and a boy. He was almost ecstatic when he learned that we also had a small grandson.

"*Na su zisi!*" he bellowed. "May he live for you!" Delving into his goatskin bag, he drew out a dubious-looking bottle from which he took a hefty swig before handing it to Harry. It looked like water, but we both knew what it was. This one had been tried on us before. It was the local firewater, *zivania,* guaranteed to clear all bronchial passages and take the enamel off your teeth.

Armed with this foreknowledge, and having been put to the test many times in the officers' mess drinking *afterburners,* Harry took a swallow without flinching. Our host looked disappointed and then offered the bottle to me, eyebrows raised hopefully. I politely declined, saying I only used it for cleaning windows.

He cackled merrily at this little jest (actually it is perfectly true - it's excellent stuff for removing greasy smears) and downed another huge swallow before putting the depleted bottle back in his bag and preparing to follow his flock. I asked him if we were near the old church, and he said it was at the bottom of the hill near the spring where he watered his sheep. We couldn't possibly miss it. He bent down to pick up a lamb that had been separated from its mother, draping it round his neck like a scarf and holding its four little legs together under his chin, before moving off along the track whistling and cajoling his flock.

We drove on to the brow of the hill and stopped. Below us we could see the watering place. Water from a natural spring flowed through a wide metal pipe which stuck out over an old-fashioned white enamelled bath. This was full to overflowing, and the overspill trickled across the track to flow on down the gentle slope towards the sea, which sparkled intensely blue against the backdrop of the Akamas mountains. Set in this lovely valley among the olive trees

71

The tiny Byzantine church of Panayia Khortani

and lush grass was the tiny Byzantine church of Panayia Hortani - Our Lady of the Grasses. The sun highlighted the mellow stones and the subtle brown tones glowed in its warmth. Dried grass grew in places around the circular domed roof and in various crevices on the outer walls. It was a scene of utter tranquillity. The cool dark interior beckoned, and we entered to see that there were still remnants of wall paintings in evidence. The colours were fairly bright, but most of the artists' work had fallen victim to damp and neglect over many years.

We sat on some large boulders near the water outlet and enjoyed our picnic, watching a variety of birds alighting on the edge of the bathtub to drink, while others bathed in the little pools which had formed below it. Once Harry had completed his photography and sketching, we retraced our route to the main road and set off to find the partly-ruined church of Ayia Ekatarini.

*****

Off the main highway and on to a dirt road once more, we drove up a narrow, steeply-winding route until, rounding a corner, we caught our breath at the first glimpse of this former monastery nestling below the hill in the distance. It was breathtakingly beautiful, with the bright noonday sun illuminating its rounded domes. It was much larger than Panayia Hortani, and had several lovely arches. Most of the wall paintings had been lost to the elements, but icons hung on the walls and people still went there to worship, particularly on St. Catherine's Day.

An old lady, clad in voluminous black, came down the track riding a grey donkey. She dismounted and greeted us warmly, taking a plastic bag from one of the pommels on the wooden saddle.

"*Ella kori,*" she said. "Come with me, my girl."

I entered the church with her and watched as she opened the

bag and took out a small bottle of oil, pouring some of it into a wide bowl set on a wooden table. She then produced a packet containing tiny wicks attached to a base which would float on the oil. She handed one to me, and together we set our little candle ships afloat. Crossing herself reverently, she lit hers and then passed me some matches. While I lit mine she moved over to the icons, which were covered with little curtains of material. Drawing back the cloth, she kissed each of them in turn, thus paying homage to St. Catherine.

Outside in the sunlight, she indicated the rugged terrain and told me that a miracle had once taken place here.

"Long ago, *kori,* the monks were in urgent need of water. Hearing their pleas, the great Dighenis himself ran down over the mountainside, leaving huge footprints which formed a deep gully so that water would flow down to the monastery."

"*O Theos een-eh Megalos,*" she said. "God is Great." With that, she remounted her patient donkey and rode off to water her *pervolia.*

*****

We drove on across undulating, unpopulated territory and followed a twisting dirt track road cut into the side of a steep-sided gorge. Tucked away near the river-bed at the bottom was a tiny church consisting of one square room with a single dome on top. This was one of the churches on our list. Its name was Ayia Paraskevi, and when Harry had finished his sketching we headed in the direction of a village, a little way up in the hills, where we had arranged to meet the priest.

His wife welcomed us warmly, bringing coffee and the traditional Cypriot *glyko* on a silver tray. The priest, whom we knew well, had told me about a rare icon of the *Panayia* which was kept

74

locked in a very old church. We were here to see it. He patted the pocket of his faded, navy-blue working robe.

"*Echo to klithi,*" he said. "*Na ba-meh?*" "I have the key. Shall we go?"

We walked the short distance to the little church, set in idyllic rural surroundings, and waited while he fitted the heavy iron key into the lock. The wooden door creaked slightly as he pushed it open, and then we were standing in the dimly-lit interior of the ancient church which was dedicated to the Archangel Michael.

He moved across to a small table set against one wall and lit a large candle, placing it in the specially designed holder. On the table, well-wrapped in a white cloth and propped against the wall, was the icon we had come to see.

The priest crossed himself and took a step forward to remove the cloth from the Holy relic. Head bowed, he stood there for a moment, obscuring our view, then stepped aside.

I found myself looking at an icon of the Virgin centred in a mounting of pure gold. The precious metal gleamed in the soft candlelight, and the flickering flame seemed to bring alive the eyes of the young woman who gazed so serenely at me from within her golden world.

I said nothing. Entranced, I could only stare and savour the moment. I glanced at the old priest. His eyes shone with unshed tears, and I knew he was deeply moved. Harry, like me, did not speak. There were no words to express what we were feeling.

We bade the old man farewell at the door of the church and drove slowly home as the shadows lengthened and the mountains took on the lilac tints of evening. We exchanged few words as we absorbed the day's events, content with a companionable silence and happy in the knowledge that we had made our home in this beautiful place.

Pyrgos tis Rigenas - the queen's tower

IN SEARCH OF A LEGEND

I got to thinking about the story the old lady had told me. The tales woven around everyday things, and accepted so naturally by the people, had long held my fascination. In all countries with a history as ancient as this, folklore and superstitions abound. The awful *Kalikantzari* are straight out of Greek mythology, while many local stories have been handed down through the generations from Pagan times. The enigmatic Akamas, however, has its own mythology, and one warm and sparkling morning, when crested larks trilled their joy of living to the world, we went in search of a legend.

Our ultimate goal was Pyrgos tis Rigenas - the Queen's tower. But who was the queen? Was she a character from local mythology, or was she indeed some mediaeval queen of Cyprus? Reality has become so mixed up with legend that it is difficult to find two stories which coincide when talking to the old men and women of the region.

Andreas, Inspector of Fisheries for the Paphos District and close friend for many years, had elected to drive. We had been on turtle watch at Lara with him countless times, and some years earlier it was he who had led us to the remote caves in the Akamas to photograph the Egyptian fruit bats. He knows every inch of the wilderness, and therefore the best routes to take to places of particular interest.

We set out in the early morning, and once out of the village and on to the dirt road that leads into the unspoilt Akamas, we found ourselves alone. No hordes of tourists, no vehicles, nor any other trappings of modern day civilisation came by to detract from the mythological world we sought to uncover. The sun shone down from a clear blue sky, and the stone walls of the little monastery of Ayios

Minas, standing in front of the mountain amid the tall pine trees, glowed in its light. A little way past the tiny building we came to Smyies, a shaded area around a natural spring. Smyies has now been transformed into an official picnic site, and the spring which formerly arose in a cave amongst huge rocks and boulders has been tamed, issuing from a pipe set in stone and concrete. Smyies comes from the Greek word meaning to join, and it was here, long ago, that two young lovers lay entwined.

The mountains on either side of us as we progressed had names relating to the mythology. Pissouros - a dark place, Skotini - another place of darkness, Kefalovrissia - a place with lots of water, Stavropiyi - a place where water flows in four directions and Sotira - a place of safety, all set fire to the imagination. Would we be able to connect these actual places with any of the myths? We had notes of the varying stories we had heard; now we would try to piece them together.

As we turned right to drive towards the extreme western point of the island, Andreas stopped the vehicle and we gazed down over sweeping, craggy escarpments to the bays and inlets of the southern coast beyond. West of the turtle hatchery at Lara two triangular rocks stood not far offshore. They were named *karavopetra,* from the Greek words *karavo* meaning sailing ship and *petra*, meaning rocks. The ancient monastery of Panayia tou Tyflou, dedicated to the blind, is situated inland of the rocks, and one day a village woman, gently smearing my eyelids with cotton wool that had been saturated with oil and candle-black from the interior walls of the tiny building, indicated the rocks and told me the story that had been handed down from mother to daughter over the centuries.

"Long ago, *kori,* the barbarian Saracens came to our shores to steal our gold, rape our daughters and destroy our churches. One night two sailing ships came close inshore under cover of darkness

He hurled a huge rock at her

and the people of Droushia and Inia were in grave danger as they slept; but the villages were protected by the Holy Virgin, and before the ships could reach land, she turned them into stone. There they stand for all to see; a reminder of the great power of good over evil.''

I stared again at the stark, black triangular sails, frozen for eternity in the warm blue waters and marvelled at the simplicity of the faith of a true believer. On westwards to look out over the lovely Fontana Amoroza and then down to the massive oak tree beside which stands Pyrgos tis Rigena - the queen's tower.

Somehow I had expected a tall building, but this was a one-roomed stone construction set amongst what appeared to be the ruins of a former monastery. Here, local legend has it, Rigena used to rest after bathing at the Baths of Aphrodite. Several villagers had told me you could still see the hole in the floor where she sat spinning and the whirling spindle had gradually worn away the stone. Her husband was Rigas, king of the Akamas region, but she had a lover, Dighenis, who pursued her relentlessly. Trying to escape his advances, she fled across the mountains. From Smyies she ran to Pissouros where the darkness covered her and he passed by without seeing her. Across the other mountains she became visible as she made for the coast where a ship was waiting to bear her away. Furious, he hurled a huge rock at her but missed. The tall rock, coloured red by the iron pyrites it contains and known as Piripetra, stands to this day below the village of Neo Khorio near the coast. Finally, she reached Sotira which slopes steeply down towards the sea, and from where she could easily leap into the water to escape him.

We explored, photographed and sketched. We saw the hole supposedly worn in the stone by the spindle and we revelled in the peace and tranquillity of the place. Moving on towards the coast,

Andreas stopped at a gully where water flowed down the mountain. Here he produced small, sweet cucumbers and ripe, red tomatoes which he washed in the spring while we listened to the chorus of bird-song and the musical splashing of the water. On down over rough and rocky terrain to an old abandoned settlement and the ruined church of Ayios Nikolaos, where vestiges of wall paintings were still visible on the walls. The land sloped gently away towards the sea, which sparkled aquamarine over the pale creamy rocks close inshore, and intensely blue further out where the water was many fathoms deep.

Andreas guided the jeep down to a small, sandy cove where we sat on the smooth rocks in the warm sunshine. He took a cold box from the back of the vehicle, and like a magician producing rabbits from a hat, brought forth newly-baked bread, *halloumi*, *kefalotiri* and ham. There was salt to go with the tomatoes and cucumbers, and fresh sweet oranges for dessert. It was a feast fit for a queen.

While we ate I looked up at Sotira, the place of safety for the queen, and pondered how the legend had arisen. Like all mythology the story differs slightly in each telling, according to the beliefs of the storyteller. Rigas and Rigena were King and Queen, but they have no names other than their royal titles. Dighenis Akritas was one of the famous heroes of mediaeval Greek legend. Revered as a hunter and protector of the open countryside, he had a habit of hurling rocks at people who upset him, and he features in much of the folk-lore of Cyprus. Perhaps the legend had been brought up to date at some point in time, and personalities to whom the people could more easily relate had been substituted for deities.

I like to believe that the original mythology concerned Adonis and Aphrodite. The immortal Goddess was born in Cyprus, off the coast of Paphos, and the site of her temple can be seen in the village of Kouklia. She was worshipped island-wide, but the sacred Baths of Aphrodite lie close to our village and it was here that she came to bathe in seclusion and meet with her lover, the beautiful youth Adonis. He used to hunt wild game on the Akamas, and Smyies, the lovely clearing in the forest where a natural spring rose among rocks surrounded with wild orchids, would have made a perfect trysting place. The whole area is noted for its spring flowers, and the beautiful scarlet poppies that abound are said to have arisen where droplets of blood fell to the ground when Adonis, gored by a wild boar, lay dying. Aphrodite, overcome with grief, wept as she made her way to the baths. And where her tears fell the delicate wild cyclamen, which bloom profusely in the region, sprang up.

Visitors who come to walk the nature trails and enjoy the unique beauty of the Akamas may find that the Goddess, so inextricably linked with this island, works her magic to lure them back again. And in springtime, passing through a land carpeted with wild anemones, cyclamen and orchids, they may feel something of what Euripides, the Greek poet who lived five centuries before Christ walked on the earth, felt when he wrote:

O to flee hence unto where Aphrodite doth in Cyprus, the paradise island, dwell.

THE MAGIC THAT IS CYPRUS

Cyprus has been seriously over-fished, and its inshore waters do not have the numbers and variety of species found in some other Mediterranean areas; but around the coast scuba divers find ancient shipwrecks to explore, as well as sea caves and sites of old sunken harbours. Turtles can be seen swimming near sandy beaches during the summer, and there is always the chance that the underwater explorer may discover something of great archaeological importance. Snorkelling, too, is fascinating in these clear unpolluted waters, and when the summer season is over and most of the sun-seekers have gone, we clean off our snorkel masks and take them with us when we go to the beach. I leave the house very early in the mornings, for I walk the two kilometres or so each day, equipped with binoculars and always dawdling, leaving Harry to follow later with the car.

Early one autumn morning I walked down through the valley to the beach at Asprokremma. The sea, pale grey and violet-hued, was calm and strangely still. Above the eastern shore the amethyst-misted mountains stretched up into a lavender sky, and westwards, Skotini, that flat-topped mountain of the Akamas, was wreathed in cloud. Banks of sea-mist rolling in obscured the far horizon and turned the sea into a shrouded lake, enchanting, cloaked in mystery. I half thought to see an arm, *clothed in white samite, mystic, wonderful,* rise up from the mirrored depths brandishing the sword Excalibur.

Pearl-drops of dew hung from long-dried grasses, and spiders' webs gleamed gossamer in the pale light. In the eerie silence sounds were somehow amplified. Way offshore I heard the voices of fishermen hauling in their nets, and from far up the mountain came

Fishermen hauling in their nets

the musical cadences of sheep bells as the flock streamed down towards the drinking troughs.

On the beach I sat atop a rock and hugged my knees, revelling in the solitude and peace. The rhythmic thrust of beating wings disturbed the air, and fifteen great white egrets flew low across the water, right in front of me. Direct, intent, in close formation they flew on through the milky luminescent dawn, their course set south. I clearly saw the snowy plumage on their breasts, the yellow bills, the black and streamlined legs, their lovely symmetry. Their beauty was perfection on this perfect morning, and my heart was filled with the magic that is Cyprus.

A sudden soft breeze stirred the air and wisps of mist curled up like smoke. Fingers of sunlight pierced the nebulous cover, casting pools of light on the still water. Soon a freshening breeze rippled over the bay to lift the last remaining haze, and as the sun's warm rays burst through, the glass-like surface of the sea shattered into sparkling fragments. The crystalline water danced under a sky of cerulean blue, and where the two met, the line of the horizon was defined in deepest indigo.

Harry came to join me and it was time to swim. The sea, late-summer warm, flowed like silk against my skin as I slid into a different world. It was as though I was in an aquarium. The sun-dappled water, still and deep, was greenly transparent, and small fish came near to inspect the intruder in their midst. Miniature forests of seaweed, growing on rocks, waved feathery branches to and fro above the sand-rippled seabed. In shallower water small pebbles lay like scattered jewels, in a marvellous array of shapes and colours. I dragged my foot through the sand, clouding the water, and at once dozens of fish swarmed around my feet eager for the unexpected feast I had disturbed for them.

The fish kept in small shoals made up of one species, although

A Kingfisher dived in

they sometimes intermingled when something interesting to eat turned up. They were completely unafraid, and as I swam they cruised along beside me like an escort of motorbikes alongside a motorcade. They followed me into the shallows when I got out of the water, and I scooped up clouds of sand and tiny pebbles for them to dart amongst.

I sat towelling my hair at the water's edge, watching Harry's bright orange snorkel tube progressing along like a periscope. Suddenly a brilliant streak of metallic blue shot along the waterline and a kingfisher dived in where I had disturbed the bottom sand for the fish. It came up with one poor victim gleaming silver in its large bill, and as was so often the case in observing wildlife, I was torn between feeling sorry for the fish and happy for the beautiful bird now perched on a nearby rock enjoying its breakfast.

A flock of thirty or so grey herons flapped slowly overhead, circling and dropping down to land on the rocky promontory, where they stood like carved statues, silhouetted against the morning sun. They were accompanied by three Little egrets with pure white plumage, black bills and legs and bright yellow feet. I have often seen them flying with the larger herons on migration, and they always seem to tag on to the end of a formation as though they are hitching a ride.

We are on one of the world's main migratory routes, and so many species pass overhead we cannot possibly identify them all. In the autumn a marvellous opportunity arises to see birds that do not normally reside here. Thousands of ducks and wading birds overfly the peninsula each year, and large flocks of cranes, many of two hundred or more birds at a time, pass directly over our house on their way south. These are the noisiest of the travellers, calling continuously to each other on their journey. Often when I hear them at night I step outside, and looking up, see them in their long V-formations crossing the moonlit sky.

Large raptors on migration are another unforgettable sight. One day, sitting on the front verandah, I saw two very big birds circling above Latchi. Reaching for the binoculars I could see they were honey buzzards, and I was disappointed when they moved inland and out of sight fairly quickly. I scanned the bay and noticed a flock of large dark-coloured birds approaching low over the water. As they came over the beach I saw that they too were buzzards, forty-five of them in all. Once over land the flock circled slowly round and round, keeping together and gradually gaining height. Then, all at once, they must have hit a thermal for they began to rise rapidly up in a funnel shape, spiralling outwards as they did so, until they peeled off at the top in ones and twos and soared inland out of sight towards the village of Droushia, situated on top of the mountain ridge that divides the north-west coast from the sea on the southern side. A few hours later I saw another flock of thirty-five buzzards do exactly the same thing in the same place.

As on other occasions when I get absorbed in the natural world around me, I didn't get much done that day; but a few cobwebs and some unwashed floors are a small price to pay for the privilege of watching these magnificent birds.

SHIPWRECKED!

One summer we bought a boat. I had been born and brought up on the Devon coast and the sea was an integral part of my life. My father had served in the Royal Navy before joining the Devon Constabulary, and he had instilled a love of the sea in both my brother and me from a very early age. My brother's prowess with a salmon rod is awesome, and there is little he does not know about the fish that inhabit the coastal waters of our native county. He made a name for himself early on as a formidable fisherman, and as well as fishing with rod and line, has always kept boats; progressing from the first minute wooden rowboat, in which we used to explore the Exe estuary, to a fast, sleek dory which he later replaced with larger fishing boats.

Harry, never a fisherman, preferred to spend his summer leisure time playing cricket - in fact we first met at a cricket match where I had turned up to cheer the opposing cleven! Now he rather fancied the idea of trolling a line through the calm waters of the bay and grilling his catch over glowing charcoal at night. It would also open up to us the Akamas coast where we had spent many glorious days, swimming and lazing in the sun in deserted bays, by getting a lift with the sponge divers. A boat of our own now seemed a logical step forward, and when the opportunity arose to acquire one from a former colleague who was posted back to the UK, we took the plunge and became the proud owners of a fourteen foot, double-skinned, fibreglass boat.

It was in beautiful condition, with a little sun-deck around which we put stainless steel rails. The steering wheel was mounted on a console, behind which the driver sat in comfort in a contoured bucket-seat. It was painted a glossy daffodil yellow and Harry sten-

One summer we bought a boat

cilled her new name, THE HAWK, and the Latchi registration number in large black letters on one side. She was a lovely sight, and we kept nipping down to the harbour to see her rocking gently at her moorings as the local fishing boats chugged by. There was, however, one slight problem. We didn't have an engine.

Originally used as a ski-boat, it had sported a powerful eighty horsepower outboard motor. We did not need anything near this capacity for our purposes, and as there was another water ski enthusiast eager to purchase it, we opted to buy just the boat and to look for a suitable outboard later on.

Now it *was* later on, and keen to get on to the high seas, we went to look at a Johnson forty horsepower outboard, described as almost new, that was for sale. It looked in good condition and we tried it out around the bay. It was more than powerful enough. In fact, if you opened it right up too quickly the bow lifted almost vertically out of the water. We handed over the money and fitted it to our new boat. We were in business at last.

We couldn't resist putting THE HAWK through her paces on the first trip out, but once we stopped trying to emulate Donald Campbell, we soon settled down to appreciate the stunning scenery around us.

Always early risers, we would have a picnic lunch packed and be down at the harbour while the first rosy flush of dawn still coloured the sky. The bay was incredibly beautiful at this time of day, and as the boat rounded the stone wall that enclosed the little harbour and turned towards the Akamas, we could see our house, most of it hidden by trees, nestling in the valley below the village. It always gave us a sense of satisfaction and achievement to see it; thankfulness too that being in the right place at the right time had enabled us to realise our dream. After years of an itinerant way of life with no permanent home, we were where we wanted to be. We had finally put down roots.

On these peerless mornings the sea was calm and unbelievably clear. I could see far down into the aquamarine depths where turtles grazed on sea-grasses and urchins spiked the rocks around the waving fronds of weed. We passed along the beach at Asprokremma and rounded the point where fresh water from the Baths of Aphrodite flowed into the sea; then along the coast where tree-clad mountains rose steeply up from the rocky shore. Goats wandered on the narrow trails, the sound of their bells carrying sweetly across the water.

Each time we made the journey there seemed to be something to delight the eye. Sometimes a small school of dolphins to escort us - the lovely streamlined forms of these superb swimmers keeping always just ahead of our bow wave; or an echelon of flying fish skimming over the water alongside, their iridescent bodies flashing in the sunlight. Often, during the latter part of the summer, large flocks of migrating birds would rise up from the small island of Ayios Giorgos as we navigated the deep water between its rocks and the shoreline; and once a flurry of blue-grey plumage caught my eye and we cut the motor to watch twelve magnificent male harriers as they took off from the pale rocks, where they had been resting, to continue their migration. As we approached the legendary Fontana Amoroza, the colour of the water, varying through emerald, aquamarine and sapphire, became a translucent turquoise through which the rippled white sand of the sea bed gleamed.

One lovely bay, which we had christened Kingfisher Bay, became our favourite stopping place. Two of these jewel-like birds were always there, streaking low across the water to dive for small fish and perching - sometimes on the rails of our boat - to preen their peacock-blue feathers in the sun. The swimming here was magnificent, in warm unpolluted water of exceptional clarity, and with no

Migrating birds would rise up from the small island

road and few boats in those days, we had the place to ourselves.

A few hundred metres away there was another bay at the back of which there was a big sea cave. There was no beach and the water was very deep. Here we would drop anchor and attach a line from the bows to the rocks, fixing a yellow and white striped umbrella to the console to provide us with shade as the morning wore on. The water was deeply turquoise over the white sand and creamy-white rocks, and snorkelling was an untold delight. We swam in around the cool, shaded interior of the sea-cave as swallows skimmed in over our heads to their nests above us. Later we would sit on the deck of our little craft, shaded by the umbrella, and eat lunch from the cold-box. It was an idyllic existence, and sometimes I felt I needed to pinch myself to make sure I wasn't dreaming.

Quite often the outboard motor would give us problems. It had never been easy to pull-start, but when it became so temperamental as not to start at all, Harry, who amongst his other qualifications has one that says he is a mechanical engineer, always managed to fix it. One day, though, having spent a leisurely morning fishing in the bay, we discovered that our almost new outboard motor was not all it purported to be. We started to head back to the harbour before the mid-day wind got up and suddenly found ourselves shipwrecked!

*****

Well I suppose shipwrecked is a bit of an exaggeration, but given that the prevailing wind was by now blowing strongly from the west and we had been trolling a line a little way north of Pomos Point, we could easily have found ourselves drifting into Turkish-occupied waters near Kokkina, the Turkish military enclave a couple of miles along the coast. We had no way of knowing whether they might take umbrage at a boat registered in the free area of Cyprus appearing on their doorstep, and blow us out of the water. Being none too keen to find out, it was all hands to the oars and pull like mad for a friendly shore.

This was not as easy as it might seem, for the oars were cumbersome great wooden things which did not want to stay in the rowlocks, and required the strength of Heracles to manipulate. In addition THE HAWK was not designed as a rowing boat, and the wind kept getting under her elevated bows and blowing us back from whence we came. Given the circumstances, though, it was row for it or abandon ship and swim for it, for the propeller of our almost new outboard had just sheared right off.

Later when a marine engineer examined it, he informed us that the motor was not reliable. We had actually worked that out for ourselves, but now we discovered that it had, as he so succinctly put it, "been for a swim". Naturally, when selling it to us, the vendor of this desirable motor had failed to mention that his boat had sunk with the outboard still on it. He had also neglected to mention that the reason it sank was because it had been driven at speed by someone with few navigational skills who had collided with a submerged rock. However, with the salt water dried out, the inside cleaned up and the outside spray-painted, it had only needed some invisible mending by the local welder on the prop shaft to render it almost new again and ready for sale. Eventually, of course, further wear and tear took its toll, and the propeller shaft sheared at the weak point, leaving us high and not so dry.

After floundering about being blown backwards and going round in circles because my pull could in no way match Harry's, we finally managed to get into the shelter of the bay on the right side of the point. We struggled on for a while, hoping to get a bit nearer to

Latchi, but it was a mammoth task wielding oars that closely resembled telegraph poles and the captain decided that the best thing was for him to stay with the ship while I got ashore and made my way back to the harbour to summon assistance.

As with all great ideas this one had one or two snags. First of all there was a fairly heavy swell by now, so in order to avoid being grounded we had to drop the anchor some way offshore. This meant I had to swim for it. Also, not realising this was going to turn into a land expedition, I had no money and no clothes other than the bikini I was wearing and a T-shirt. Still, our humble craft not being equipped with ship to shore radio and there being no other boats in view, there was nothing left but to get on with it.

Having commandeered Harry's T-shirt, which was considerably larger than mine and would therefore cover up quite a lot of me, I dived in and trod water while he tied it inside a plastic bag to keep it dry. Great, now I only had one arm to swim with. But my captain quickly pooh-poohed any notion that this slight handicap might pose any problem.

"You swam clear across the Exe estuary the first time they let women in that race," he said. "If you can do that you can do this with both legs tied together; besides, you taught that one-armed bloke to swim in your beginners' class at Bingham - and *he* had asthma."

My confidence bolstered by this reminder of my swimming prowess in the distant past, and grateful not to be suffering from asthma, I struck out for the shore - my head underwater most of the way as I waved the plastic bag aloft in an attempt to keep the T-shirt dry.

I reached the beach and sat recovering my breath and drying off in the sun, while the boat bobbed around like a cork and Harry shouted instructions (or something) to me, which I couldn't hear anyway because of the noise of the waves breaking. Pulling on the T-shirt, which had looked so roomy compared with mine but which now seemed to be decidedly skimpy, I trudged up the beach until I came to the long, straight main road that runs between Polis and Pomos. There I stood, barefoot, bedraggled and somewhat inadequately dressed, feeling like an idiot.

I desperately hoped the first car along would be driven by tourists or someone who didn't know me. No such luck. The only car to come skidding to a stop was driven by an incredulous Savvas, one of the men who regularly delivered building materials to our house. He was an engaging character, though, and when I explained my predicament and indicated Harry stuck out at sea, he cordially invited me to get into his car. It would be his great pleasure to take me to the harbour.

To say that his car had seen better days was a bit of an understatement. It looked as though he had raced it in a Demolition Derby - and lost. To add to my discomfort his grin, already stretching from ear to ear, widened perceptibly as my too-short T-shirt got even shorter when I sat in the passenger seat.

Once back at Latchi, however, help was quickly available from the fishermen, and I was soon clambering into a boat and heading towards Harry to tow him into the safety of the harbour.

*****

A couple of weeks later, equipped with a new outboard, we were back in business. Andreas the Turtle fixed Harry up with a shallow round fishing basket in which a long line was coiled. This had hooks with tiny lures attached, and while I steered the boat around at a moderate speed, Harry played out his line behind the boat. We

97

spent many carefree hours in this pursuit and caught more fish than we had previously done using live bait. It wasn't as smelly either.

I look back on those truly halcyon days now with a tinge of regret that we no longer have THE HAWK. The truth is, though, that after a couple of years of blissful excursions with the high seas more or less to ourselves, we realised that our boating days were numbered. The local population was becoming more affluent and acquiring speedboats which were moored at Latchi, and pleasure boats carrying crowds of tourists plied to and fro along the coast. There were water-skiers and wind-surfers and people dangling from parachutes being towed along. It was getting pretty crowded in the summer months, and when, finally, access along the coastal rock road opened up as more and more people acquired four-wheel-drive vehicles, we decided we would retire from the boating fraternity. That autumn we sold THE HAWK and began to build the swimming-pool.

IT'S MY TURN TO BAT

Snow fell on the Troodos mountains in late November, and the weather down here turned colder. We kept a blazing log fire going in the living-room, and once again I was glad to have a wardrobe full of tights, leg-warmers and tracksuits from my days of teaching physical education. It was warm and comfortable apparel, and the thick-soled training shoes kept my feet from coming in contact with the marble tiles which, though cool and smooth in summer, are decidedly chilly underfoot in winter.

One morning some weeks later, I was brushing fallen leaves from the pool-side, and not for the first time noticed several large splashes of what looked like liquid mud on the flagstones. Neither of us could come up with a feasible idea as to how they came to be there. It looked a little as though swallows, having picked up soil for nesting, had swooped into the pool to take in water and dropped splashes of wet mud as they overflew the patios. But there were no swallows here in winter, and in any case these mysterious splashes were appearing at night. Definitely not owls - they did not drop anything resembling the marks, and there were a great many of these splodges around the pool. Rats, hedgehogs etc. were all ruled out as there were no footprints. This was something being dropped from above. The small bats, which flit so numerously over the pool in summer, had long since gone into hibernation. Then we began to find carobs, showing the marks of small, sharp teeth, lying on the patios or floating in the pool. We were at a loss for an explanation.

Harry put some new batteries in a powerful halogen torch one night and went out by the pool every hour or so up until midnight to investigate. Nothing - and no new splashes appeared during that time. We went to bed still mystified.

In the morning there were lots more splashes, some stretched out in long lines. This was ridiculous. I determined to find out what was the cause, even if I had to stay awake all night.

I almost did. When at eleven o'clock the following night Harry said there was nothing to report, I pulled on extra leg-warmers, a scarf and a thick jacket, and leaving my spouse to the comfort of the crackling pine-logs, I stepped outside the downstairs bedroom door. There I sat, clutching the powerful flashlight, in under the arched verandah that overlooks the swimming-pool.

An hour passed and nothing happened. Harry came down and, realising I was determined to stick it out, kissed me goodnight and went to bed. Another hour passed. I was freezing and thought enviously of him snuggled warmly under the feather duvet.

Outside, my cold world was stunningly beautiful. The moon had risen, silvering the still surface of the water, and the infinite sky was resplendent with scintillating stars.

The silence was abruptly broken soon after one o'clock. I heard a sound like a wet towel flapping and something big flew in under the arches just above my head, causing me to duck and almost fall off the chair. It turned at the end of the pool and dived down, hitting the water with an audible `splosh', before pulling up and cannoning into the carob trees above the shower. I shone the torch into the trees and there, hanging upside down from a branch, was a large fruit bat. I directed the beam to the pool-side and there were more of the splashes, freshly made and glistening in the torchlight.

I could scarcely believe my eyes. The fruit bats were eating carobs, and at a time when we had presumed them to be hibernating. As I stood there slowly absorbing this information, another one zoomed in over the studio roof and straight into the trees. I jumped

Hanging upside down from a branch

again as yet another rounded the side of the house, lined up at the end of the pool and hit the surface of the water, before flying noisily up, leaving more of the tell-tale brown splashes in its wake.

I instantly realised that these creatures were ravenously hungry. Their preference is for soft fruits like *mespila,* apricots, peaches and grapes, but with nothing like these available at this time of the year, they were feeding on the previous season's unharvested carobs. The black pods, although sweet and extremely nutritious, are obviously not as palatable to the *niktokorakos* as are the soft fruits of summer, so they were taking water from the pool to help soften them. The brown stains came from carob juice dripping from their mouths as they swooped over the pool-side.

I was amazed, but also pleased to be unwittingly playing host to these unique bats. I had seen them many times purloining fruit in the village, and once we had gone on an expedition to photograph them in the deep caves they inhabit in an inaccessible gorge in the Akamas. This was the first time I had seen them here at the house, however, but it was certainly not to be the last.

Cold and tired but, once again, lifted up by the wonders to be encountered in this rugged place, I climbed under the duvet, and folding myself around Harry's warmth, fell quickly into a dreamless sleep.

ORCHID GEORGE

Spring rapidly follows autumn in Cyprus; sometimes you don't even realise that winter has been and gone until you see the first of the early flowers appearing.

One February morning a stranger came to the door. He apologised for the intrusion and said he was in the area searching for a rare orchid which, apparently, grew only in Cyprus and in Syria. He turned out to be a bit of an expert on wild orchids, in fact they were his passion. He introduced himself as George - for ever after to be known as Orchid George - and he came from Harry's home town of Exeter.

The orchid he was seeking, *Orchis punctulata,* was on record at Kew as being one plant "somewhere between Latchi and the village of Neo Khorio''. He had been making enquiries down at Latchi and they had sent him to me, saying that Sheila liked flowers and birds and would know for sure where to find the mystery plant.

He smiled encouragingly at me.

"But I hardly know the difference between an orchid and a tulip.'' I protested.

"Ah, but you know the area. You can't possibly mistake this one once I've described it for you. It's a big, showy orchid. It will stand up and say 'hello' when you see it.''

I considered the task. There were acres of uncultivated fields and scrub between here and Latchi, much of it grazed by sheep and goats. Finding one single flower would be, quite literally, like looking for the proverbial needle in a haystack.

I poured us both a cup of coffee while my unexpected guest waxed poetic about this strikingly beautiful yellow flower. He had the unbridled optimism of the true enthusiast, and he was determined to find the elusive plant. His time on the island was limited. Would I please help him in his quest?

My heart was not really in it, for I considered we would be taking on an impossible task. But he was desperately keen and it was a lovely day for a walk anyway. Before I knew it I was rinsing the coffee cups and reaching for my boots and the stout stick - useful when encountering sleepy snakes - which always stands by the front door. I asked where the plant was most likely to grow. Near the sea? In a meadow? On a mountain?

"On a north-facing slope," he replied instantly.

I racked my brains as we walked along and, from the dark recesses of my memory, a half-remembered conversation with one of the village landowners came back. He told me some foreign botanists had once come to photograph a flower that grew on his land.

"Can you believe it, *kori*, they came all this way to see something you can't even eat?"

His land was not too far away, and I knew that one boundary stretched across the top of a very steep hill that faced north towards Turkey.

We tramped through long wet grass and prickly scrub; we clambered over stone walls and climbed rocky slopes. Nothing was too much trouble for George in pursuit of his dream.

When we reached the foot of the steep-sided hill where I had decided to start our search, Orchid George, in his eagerness, was ahead of me. Suddenly he leapt back and I saw a black snake, which had been sunning itself on a rock, slither by his foot as it made for cover at our approach. It was only about a metre long and quite harmless, but the confrontation calmed him down a bit, and as we began to climb up I found I was leading the way.

"Lots of cistus," said George approvingly. "That's always a good indication there are orchids about."

Soon he was pointing out various species of orchid. I could not understand how I had missed seeing these fascinating plants before. I suppose it just needed someone to open my eyes, and who better than someone with the enthusiasm and knowledge of Orchid George? He was a mine of information, and later backed it up with books and references, leaving me with a wealth of stuff to study on the wild orchids of Cyprus.

We reached a point about half-way up the steeply-sloping field, where an old stone wall had collapsed. I sat down on a rock to rest while George scurried about the hillside, hell-bent on finding this rare plant. I glanced down at the ground. Just by my left foot some-one had erected a small cairn from some of the fallen stones, and in the centre, protected on all sides, was a tall flower spike, the petals of which were not yet fully open. It looked to be mainly green, but the topmost petals had a definite yellow tinge about them. I stood up.

"George, come and have a look at this."

He came haring back to where I was pointing with my stick, and a rapturous smile broke out on his face. He linked his arm in mine and we danced a little jig around one way and then the other.

"You actually found it!" he said incredulously.

I have to admit I was pretty astounded myself. I had thought initially that we'd have been better off trying to find something easy like the Holy Grail. I did not think there was any real possibility of finding it. But here I was, dancing a jig on a deserted hillside with a complete stranger, because we had!

"It's not open yet," said George. "But a few more sunny

The rare Orchis punctulata

days like this and it will be in full bloom.''

He knelt down.

"I'll just take a few photographs while we're here.''

A *few* photographs? He had more camera equipment than 20th Century Fox, and he photographed that plant from every angle. He had things to measure the light and reflectors to give more light. He had lenses for every occasion and he used all of them. He finished his film and he put in another. He took so many pictures he could have written a book on a thousand and one ways to photograph an orchid. Orchid George was a happy man.

He was staying in Paphos, and for the next two days I drove him around in our 4 x 4 jeep seeking out wild orchids. He taught me how to find and identify the ones growing in this region, and I will always be grateful to him for introducing me to the incredible world of this marvellous species.

When we returned to the rare *Orchis punctulata* a few days later, it was to find the tall, sturdy plant in full and glorious flower in the spring sunshine. Golden yellow and unbelievably beautiful, it stood alone in the shelter of the little stone cairn. We simply sat there awhile drinking in its beauty, then I sneaked away and left him alone to photograph it, for I knew only too well how long *that* was going to take.

*****

When Orchid George finally left the island I got to thinking that there must surely be more of these plants in the area. It did not seem feasible for there to be only the one, so in the next few days, I walked a grid system over the surrounding hills and found another twenty-five specimens. I asked everyone who owned fields near us whether they knew of this special flower and it was here, in search of the elusive *Orchis punctulata,* that I had my first major failure in pursuance of the Greek language.

Having heard that one of the village worthies had big yellow flowers growing on his land, I asked a bemused septuagenarian if he would take me to his field and show me his orchids. I was rather proud of my fluent use of the plural *orchidae* and totally unaware that in Greek it means testicles.

He batted not an eyelid as he politely replied: "*Avrio, koukla mou,* it will be my great pleasure." But I swear he sat up straighter on his donkey as they plodded on down the lane.

SOMEWHERE THERE'S A GOD
CALLED MURPHY

Murphy's Law - anything that can go wrong will go wrong.

One spring, when the orchids were in bloom, we began to think about the hot weather approaching and long days to be spent sunning and swimming. It was time to repaint the pool. Five years on, the rich colour had faded to a washed-out blue, and the protective coating was wearing thin in places. The memory of some of the traumas we had faced in applying it for the first time had faded with the paint. So ever the optimists, we handed over the king's ransom demanded by the suppliers, and armed with several containers of epoxy resins and tins of hardener, we set about devising a master-plan for the transformation of our pool.

At this stage it was free of chlorine, and to avoid undue wear and tear on the pump, we rigged up a hosepipe to siphon the water into the *argaki* which runs through our land. As it drained slowly away we worked out stage two of our plan. We would have to get the top layer of old paint off before we could apply the primer, so Harry ferreted around in the garden shed checking over angle-grinders and sanders. By bedtime the water level had dropped considerably - totally confusing Botham (the opening bat) who had to make two or three passes before he managed to get a drink. We went to bed satisfied with the day's progress.

During the night we were woken by a violent electrical storm followed by torrential rain and, in the morning, the level of the pool had risen to where it was before we started siphoning.

Well used to these minor setbacks, we left the hosepipe in place and carried on with other tasks. Of course it continued to rain heavily for days, but eventually the clouds passed and the water level slowly sank until, one morning when we went out, the pool was empty.

Having received explicit instructions on how to proceed when it was my turn to scrape the paint off, I was eager to get on with it - convinced that with two of us working in there the job would be over in no time. Dressed in protective clothing, including a particle mask against the blue dust and ear-defenders against the deafening noise of the angle-grinder, I looked like some giant insect as I descended into the pit. Once there my spirits sank faster than the water level had done. Devoid of water and with every inch of the walls and floor needing to be cleared of paint, our nine-by-five-metre pool suddenly took on all the dimensions of an Olympic arena. It was going to take forever to get this lot off.

The weather remained unsettled and we alternated between bailing out the pool, scraping paint off the walls, and wondering whether we would finish it this century. Then we received a telephone call from a friend at the British Base at Episkopi.

The Hash House Harriers were coming to Latchi to run on the Akamas and would be staying, with their families, for a long weekend in various rented villas near us. Knowing that Harry was not completely fit, having recently had surgery, they were coming here on the Saturday morning to give him a hand with any heavy work that needed doing.

What an answer to a prayer! The hares, who were laying the trail for the evening run, loaded up stuff that was waiting to be removed to the local refuse dump, while the main body of runners, kitted up with masks and ear-defenders, got down into the pit and started grinding. The noise was unbelievable - like a squadron of German stukas screaming in on a low level raid - but the blue dust flew and the walls became barer by the minute. As the faded paint

I looked like some giant insect

disappeared, hundreds of black spots appeared all over the surface. We were uncovering the desiccated corpses of swarms of flies which had embedded themselves in the first layer of paint when we had originally built the pool.

Every now and then work came to a halt and the team sat on a wall, looking like aliens from another planet in their protective clothing, while Harry poured them cold beer from the studio fridge. We still have the warm feeling that enveloped us to know that these caring men willingly gave up part of their special weekend to give us a helping hand.

With very little left to scrape off in the ensuing day or so, Harry still managed to whip the revolving disk of an angle-grinder across the back of his hand, necessitating a trip to the local hospital for some stitches and a tetanus injection.

Finally all was ready for the start of stage three of the master-plan, and at this point, of course, the weather broke. We had thunder, lightning, hail and torrential rain accompanied by high winds. We stuck the siphon back in the pool and waited.

Stage three was to apply the resin primer, and for this we needed a couple of days when we could be sure it would not rain. No problem, we thought, for we had hi-tech satellite information on the weather telephoned in by friends, from CNN, NBC, Euronews, TV5 from France, Cyprus Broadcasting and the Met. Office at Akrotiri. Unfortunately these forecasts never coincided; we began to get slightly paranoid, and missed a couple of opportunities when we could have done it safely. Eventually, when four out of six were vaguely similar one morning, we rushed out and scanned the skies over the Akamas for rain clouds. There were none. The sky was clear and blue, and as we stood there anxiously gazing skywards, we were opportunely presented with irrefutable evidence that it was not going to rain. A steady rumble of curses and admonitions heralded the arrival of Theodoulos with his donkey train, and as he passed us we saw he was wearing his wide-brimmed bright orange sun-hat! We got out the paint and started mixing.

*****

Days earlier, in anticipation of painting, we had taken the precaution of bringing several heavy planks into position around the pool. These were needed to hold down a huge net under which we could work without getting millions of flies and clouds of dust stuck in the paint before it had time to dry. We climbed down into the pit, pulling the net over us, and got to work. It was hard going. The resin, when mixed, closely resembled bread dough that had been dipped in water. It was a while before we got the knack of getting just the right amount of moisture on the walls to brush it on evenly. At lunchtime we had finished and the sun was still shining. We flopped into some easy chairs and opened a bottle of wine.

The Gods were kind to us. The glorious weather held, and two days later with the sealant hardened to a glass-like surface, we climbed into the pit once more - this time to apply the beautiful blue finishing coat. This was a lot easier. The thick, creamy paint slid on, covering all the unsightly marks and scratches we had made with the angle-grinders. It was hot and tiring down there under the net, and when we reached the final corner where the ladder stood for us to get out, we were both pretty exhausted. I went up first and Harry handed me all the equipment before painting his way as far as he could - leaving one last footprint, and the marks that would be left when we pulled up the ladder, to be covered over. He handed me his brush and started to climb up.

This was when we realised that, somewhere up on Mount

Olympus, there must be a God called Murphy who has a hand in our affairs. Harry had one hand on the top rung and one on the poolside, just about to transfer his weight on to solid ground, when the ladder disappeared, taking him with it. It all happened so quickly I could only look on in horror, praying that his replacement hip joint, which had taken four hours of painstaking surgery to put in place, had not moved down to become an ankle joint in four seconds. I needn't have worried. Tough as ever, he only had a few bruises to show for it - plus, of course, most of the paint we had just put on the floor and which now adorned him from head to foot.

In retrospect I must say he did it with a great deal of panache. The ladder skidded through the wet paint like a sledge on the Cresta Run, with Harry right behind it. He went at such a speed he could have taken the Gold Medal in the one-man luge. Then came the really tricky bit. He tried to stand up, but he was on a glassy smooth surface which had just been covered in thick slippery paint, and he flailed and slid around with no chance of getting any purchase. He was trapped and the ladder was down there with him.

Speed was of the essence. This epoxy was supposedly quick-drying, so we had to repaint all the area that had been wiped off and get him out of there before he became a permanent decoration on the bottom of the pool. I needed to come up with another of my bright ideas. There was no time for finesse or intricate planning. I threw in the towel - literally. To be accurate, several of them: small hand towels which he could use as stepping-stones to keep his footing and paint his way back into the corner. Two more went under the feet of the ladder to stop it slipping as he climbed up; then it only remained for him to tie the paint brush to a broom-handle and, from a prone position, cover over the last marks before submitting to my lengthy and somewhat painful ministrations as I tried to scrub the blue paint off him as quickly as possible.

*****

A week later, having filled the pool, we prepared to add the chemicals that would make it safe for swimming. Murphy hadn't finished with us, though, and having spilt a pool of concentrated chlorine solution on the pool-side as he mixed, Harry somehow contrived to sit in it, wearing only a brief pair of swimming trunks. A week earlier his bottom had been a glorious blue. Now it turned a vivid scarlet. He was due a second tetanus jab from the first mishap with the angle-grinder, so when we went to the little local hospital that day, we mentioned the problem to the duty nurse. I don't think she had seen anything like it before, and after gazing incredulously for a moment at his technicolour behind, she called for the doctor to take a look. It gave her a bit of a surprise too, but she quickly gave him a cortisone injection and prescribed anti-histamine tablets and cream, and once again he had to suffer the indignity of my close attention to his nether regions.

For my part I must say I now find his routine skin-colour bottom a bit boring. I can hardly wait to see what colour he will turn it next.

WARBLERS AND WHEATEARS

Spring wore on, and the Scops owls, who had been silent for a few months, began softly calling to each other and periodically visiting their nest box on the front verandah. As the weeks passed they would make more frequent visits, becoming ever more vociferous, until the eggs were laid during the first week of May. From then on the female would stay in the box, leaving only for very short periods at night to hunt for food in the garden below.

Other birds, too, were beginning to think about nesting. Harry called me one day to see something in a section of the rosemary hedge. When I peered in it was to see a tiny pair of eyes solemnly regarding me. A small, dark-headed bird was sitting in a nest which had been built no more than a metre above the ground. The bird appeared unafraid and did not move. Some time later I looked again and saw that the nest was empty. Moreover, I noted that it was an old one from the previous year and had a sizeable hole in the base. I was rather disappointed, having thought we were about to acquire some more lodgers. We already had the Scops owls in a nest box on the front verandah and the Cyprus pied wheatears in another on the studio wall. I was hoping we might have a pair of Cyprus warblers (that attractive little bird, with the black barring on its breast, which appears on the Cyprus ten pound note) moving in too. Suddenly the bird appeared again, flying past me to land on a fence-post before disappearing into the bush and resettling itself on the nest.

Now my curiosity was really aroused, for it was a Sardinian warbler, identifiable by its bright red eye-ring and plain, pale breast. In addition it was a male, yet here it was, seemingly unworried by

The male bird would immediately settle himself on the eggs

my presence, flitting in and out of the bush and sitting in an old nest.

This was an ideal opportunity to observe the bird at close quarters. At that time, ornithologists had no record of Sardinian warblers actually breeding here in Cyprus. They were marked as being winter visitors or passage migrants. I was convinced they did breed here, though, having seen a pair of them in and around the garden from February onwards in previous years. They were avid purloiners of the sweet, black berries produced by the lantana bushes we had planted.

It was a day or two later before I checked again. The nest was empty, but the hole had been skilfully repaired and fresh material had been woven into the sides. From then on the male and the browner female were never far from the site, and one day when I looked in there were four eggs in the nest. The female did most of the sitting, but when she left for any length of time, the male bird would immediately settle himself on the eggs. They had become so used to us that, even when I was watering the fruit trees and standing within a couple of feet of the nest, they did not fly off, nor did they make any kind if warning noise.

One of them still stayed in the nest even when the eggs had hatched, for these small birds are nidicolous, although they would sometimes leave it to search for food if the day was warm and sunny. Then I was able to look in and see that the newly-hatched young resembled little brown worms, having no feathers and unopened eyes. It was truly amazing to watch the parent birds feeding minute flies to these chicks. They had infinite patience and pushed the food into the tiny gapes with the utmost gentleness. Sometimes one bird would perch on the fence, with food in its beak, having to wait ages for its mate to finish feeding the young before it could offer its own contribution.

As the chicks increased in size, so too did the amounts of

food they were given, and Harry took some good slides of the male bird, perched on the fence post with a fat green caterpillar in its mouth, patiently waiting its turn to feed the nestlings.

They raised three healthy fledglings who followed the male bird around like shadows once they got airborne. He simply couldn't get away from them. Later the adults had another shot at parenthood, laying four more eggs and, once again, raising three beautiful baby Sardinian warblers. In our garden they now outnumber the Cyprus warblers, and appear to be going from strength to strength.

*****

That same spring the little black and white Cyprus pied wheatears, who have nested in a box on the studio wall for some years, were a bit put out. Having built a new barbecue pit fairly near them, Harry decided to move their nest box a few metres away up in under the sloping roof of the wooden carport. It was an ideal location - sheltered from the wind and rain and shaded from the burning sun. There was, however, one small problem. They did not like it.

The female flew in and out of the studio, scolding loudly, and refused to use the custom-made box she had used for years. Eventually, obviously in high dudgeon, they nested in a hole in the rock face more than a hundred metres away and managed to raise only one chick.

I felt terrible for so cursorily evicting them, and persuaded Harry to fix the box to a beam in under the arches of the verandah outside our bedroom. I knew they would raise a second brood, and hoped they would use the box again and forgive me.

It sat there, with their own beautifully constructed little nest tucked inside it, for a couple of weeks. Then, suddenly, the female began zooming in with her beak full of dried grass and leaves. She came in and out almost non-stop, but inexplicably piled it on *top* of the box. Inexplicably because the box had a sloping roof, and as soon as she had accumulated a certain amount, predictably, it slid off. This did not deter her and she carried on bringing more and more material, most of which ended up on the floor.

These birds breed only in Cyprus and nearly always nest in holes, but this one seemed determined to ignore her own nest inside the box and make a new one on top with the verandah ceiling six inches or so above it.

Given the angle of inclination of the roof, though, there was no way she could be successful. She needed something to counter the effect of gravity. Improvising with some black tape and a few draw-ing-pins, we hastily attached a strip of plywood across the front of the box to halt the slide.

She quickly filled all the available space with dried leaves and flower petals, and then proceeded to weave her little nest on top. Before long she was contentedly sitting on her second clutch of eggs.

Roughly a fortnight later she had hatched four beautiful chicks, and we were somewhat inconvenienced by having the adult birds streaking across the verandah all day to feed them.

This was more than compensated for by the fact that, for the first time, we were really able to see the development of the young birds. In previous years they had always been well-hidden inside the box until they were ready to fly. Now, we could not only see them clearly but photograph them as well.

In comparison with the male Sardinian warbler, this male was not such an outstanding parent. He did not participate in the nest-building and, although he brought food regularly, he spent consider-ably less time with the nestlings than did his mate, who even roost-

She hatched four beautiful chicks

ed on the box every night until they were ready to leave. This, however, was when he really came into his own, for he was a fierce and fearless defender of his young.

When the fledglings were almost ready to go we became anxious that the rather flimsy strip of plywood, which held the whole nest in position, would give way as they moved about eagerly clamouring for food and vigorously fluttering their wings. But, happily, it all held together.

Then one night, shortly before dusk, Harry went out to shut up the studio and spotted one of the baby birds floating in the swimming-pool. He immediately fished it out and called for assistance. I found a small wicker basket and, while Harry filled it with dried flower petals and soft grass, I cupped the tiny creature in the palms of my hands to keep it warm. It shivered, but seemed quite bright and unafraid. Luckily its feathers were not totally saturated, and I put it in the centre of the basket and pulled the soft, dried material over it, almost completely covering it, for the air temperature would soon drop. We then placed it on the window-sill below the nest which, thankfully, still had the other three young ones snuggled in it.

In the morning the sun was already up when we woke and all four fledglings had gone. It was not difficult to locate the general area where one or the other of them was hidden at any given time, as the parents, uttering agitated warning cries, overflew them or perched above them, bringing food and ferociously driving off predators. Every now and then a tiny dark brown and white baby would fly a metre or two, low over the ground, as one of the parents called it to fresh cover. We prayed that Oscar (our resident black snake) would not show up for a few days until they could get really airborne, and we kept our eyes open for wild cats. Apart from that we just had to leave them to get on with it.

This they did, and several weeks later at least three fully fledged little pied wheatears were happily installed in the garden, feeding on the sweet black berries of the lantana bushes.

LIVING WITH AN OWL

The Scops owl population is doing well around us too. They usually manage to raise at least two and sometimes three young ones. This year they produced four, although the fourth one nearly didn't make it.

Their breeding season had followed the normal pattern, and once the eggs had hatched, both birds were busy soon after dusk each night hunting for food. As the chicks grew bigger, they began to bring food even before darkness fell, flying almost continuously over our heads, and we realised that they must have quite a large family.

The first chick appeared on the ledge of the box one evening, soon to be joined by a second. They were a strong and healthy little pair and obviously very well-fed. The female now took to roosting in a cypress tree a few metres away; it looked as though it was getting a bit crowded in the box, and the days were getting hotter. The first two, whom we called the terrible twins, then became more adventurous and leapt off the box on to the white trellis. We have trained purple bougainvillaea around the area, together with a beautiful sweet-smelling stephanotis which climbs up and twines around the woodwork, and they hopped and leapt around there exercising their wings. A third chick appeared on the ledge of the box from time to time, but it was slightly smaller than the others and did not have the confidence to leave the nest. The parents fed the twins outside but still carried on dropping food into the box.

They always know when it is time for their offspring to fly. They begin stoking them up with masses of food very early on in the evening, then sit in the trees opposite calling repeatedly until the fledglings eventually take the plunge into space and follow them into the trees. This is when the situation becomes a bit frantic for them; they have to chase around and keep their eyes on the ones who have gone and are unable to feed themselves, yet still find time to bring food for any others in the nest box and encourage them to leave too. A day after the first two had flown, the third one jumped on to the trellis, and later that night it took off and managed to reach the trees. The adults were still bringing food to the box, so we knew there was at least one more inside, but it did not show itself on the ledge.

The next night the parents, who were rushing around after the first three, came only intermittently to the box and then stopped bringing food. We thought that perhaps we might have a deformed owlet in there, and as is usually the case in nature, we would see the survival of the fittest. The adult birds had enough on their hands with three healthy fledglings to raise. If the fourth was not strong enough to leave the nest under its own steam, we knew they would abandon it.

They did. The following morning we could hear feeble movements in the box, and once or twice I saw a wing-tip raised up in the entrance. But the bird was obviously not able to get up on to the ledge. The day got hotter and the movements ceased. It was now or never, so Harry put his hand in the box and handed me a pathetically tiny, weightless bundle of damp feathers. The owlet's head lolled limply to one side and its eyes were closed. I stole - not for the first time - one of Harry's best sable paintbrushes, dipped it in some water and gently brushed it along the side of the little beak. Immediately one eye opened. There was hope yet! I persevered with the water, and before long the other eye opened and the head came up to look around.

I laid the little owl in a basket while I mixed some raw chicken liver and egg yolk into a pulpy mess. It watched me from the depths of the basket without moving, but when I reached in to pick

A totally crestfallen Johnny

125

it up again it clicked loudly and glared at me indignantly. The tiny creature was exceedingly hungry, though, and when I offered the paintbrush with the gooey glob of food it lunged forward and gulped it down right away. After two or three big swallows it began to take an interest in its surroundings and was able to stand, unaided, on my hand. I inspected the owlet thoroughly. The downy baby feathers were a pale silvery-grey with white markings, and although only about half the size of the first two fledglings, it was perfect in every way. It regarded me solemnly, obviously having decided I was a good source of nourishment, and stopped telling me off. Now when I picked up the paintbrush, it made the little purring noise the young always make when the parents bring them food.

I brushed its feathers gently with a dry toothbrush and put it back in the basket - the same basket we had used for Johnny, the deformed baby Scops owl who had been abandoned in the nest box a few years earlier. There was nothing deformed about this one, though, and I had high hopes of getting it back into the wild once it was strong enough to fly.

*****

The collective colloquial name given to the owls by the villagers being 'Johnny', we opted to call this little owlet 'Johnny' too. Dedicated as I am to the preservation of wildlife, there was no way I was going to wake up three or four times a night to feed the new baby, so he had to adapt to being fed throughout the day. He never refused food when it was offered, and grew in leaps and bounds.

Owls, like other birds of prey, need to cast pellets to remain healthy, so somehow or other I had to get some of his natural food in his diet. These small owls mainly eat large insects, and luckily for

126

us this was a fourth year when hundreds of cicadas were emerging from below ground and metamorphosing into large, winged, and very noisy insects. When people came to visit us we handed them a net attached to the end of a bamboo pole, and they weren't allowed to have a drink until they had caught at least two cabbage white butterflies or a cicada. Anyone who landed a nice leggy grasshopper got to go and pour their own right away, while the little owl got to dine on liver and egg yolk garnished with grasshopper legs.

When he had been fed for the last time at night he was, of course, very active and wide awake. He would run and hop along the backs of the chairs and perch on our shoulders while we watched the television news. He loved to run along the back of the settee, and as the nights went by he became more venturesome, beginning to take flying leaps from one piece of furniture to the next.

I brought a wooden clothes horse upstairs and he spent ages perched on it or messing about getting from one level to the next.

"For God's sake, Johnny, go and play on the airer."

This became a frequent plea as Harry, trying to watch a televised football match, suffered the consequences of being in the way when the little owl decided to run the gamut of the living-room furniture. Starting at the top of an armchair he would run along the back, leap the space to the next one and run along that, leap on to the sofa, where he had a really long run before leaping on to the last armchair in which Harry was sitting. Johnny couldn't stand not being able to get right to the end of the line, so he'd run on to Harry's shoulder, hop on top of his head and down on to the other shoulder to reach the end of the last chair. Then of course he had to go all the way back again. If Harry objected vocally to this treatment, a totally crestfallen Johnny would rush over to stand on me, staring reproachfully at his critic and making him feel a complete

127

rotter.

"You've taught him to feed himself. I wish you'd teach the blighter to fly," said Harry, as he was trampled on for the umpteenth time one night.

Well, the day was not far off. I was slowly preparing him for survival in the outside world. Having got him to take food by himself, instead of having to feed him with the brush, I was introducing into his diet some of the live insects he would catch for himself when he went solo.

*****

He now preferred to sit on a perch to roost by day, so we made him a tree by wiring a leafy carob branch to the clothes horse. When we went to bed we left him in the spare bedroom, having covered the furniture with old sheets. Here he could practise flying short distances and exercise his newly-fledged wings. In the mornings he would be roosting up against the upright centre pole of the clothes airer, half-hidden in his makeshift tree.

I was torn between setting him free, so that he would not become too dependent on us, and waiting until I felt he could fly well enough to have a fighting chance of survival. For unlike the others, he would not have the adult birds to teach him how to hunt. With this uppermost in my mind, every day I made careful note of his prowess in the air.

One evening, ten days after we had taken him from the box, he flew the length of the living-room. He was a strong, sturdy little owl with beautiful golden-yellow eyes and tiny raised ear tufts. He managed the length of the room again without doing a nose-dive, and I determined that the following day I would feed him up well and

Roosting in his clothes - horse tree

release him soon after dusk fell.

Day eleven dawned, and when I went in to see him, he flew a complete circuit of the spare bedroom before landing on my shoulder. A friend, who had been filming him every few days, took some last shots of him eating and roosting in his clothes-horse tree. Then he put away his camcorder and helped us hunt for insects to keep 'on the hoof' until it was time for Johnny's last supper with us.

I would be untruthful if I said I had not become very attached to this endearing little character, but he belonged in the wild and I was going to give him every chance to succeed there if I could.

I fed him just before it got dark, and then opened the big sliding windows to the upstairs front verandah. The adult birds were calling to each other further down the valley, and he listened intently, turning his head towards the sound. I put him in his basket, leaving it uncovered, and hung it on a hook underneath the nest box. He stayed there chucking softly while we sat back at the end of the patio, watching and waiting.

I could hardly believe what happened next. I heard more chucking, and when we directed a beam of light across to the cypress trees opposite, two baby Scops owls were sitting, one above the other, answering his calls.

He became agitated and excited, and came up to perch on the edge of the basket. He then, fairly quickly, pulled himself up through the bougainvillaea on to the trellis. No adult owls appeared and I could not see the third owlet in the trees.

He began leaping around and flapping his wings, then suddenly launched himself into space and landed on the solar heater gantry between the house and the trees. He stayed there for a few minutes, then lifted off and flew the short distance into the cypress trees to join the others.

I felt at once elated and downcast. I couldn't bear to see him go, but for him to make it to the trees and have his siblings waiting for him was way beyond my expectations.

Every year, about seven to ten days after they leave the nest box, the fledglings return to the verandah alone. One year our son, who was here on holiday for a few weeks, was sitting on the verandah with his legs stretched out on another chair, drinking a cup of coffee. To his immense surprise and delight a baby owl suddenly flew over the balcony rail and landed on his leg where it sat, quite unconcernedly, for a few minutes before taking off again. We have always assumed that after a week or so the adults leave the fledglings to fend for themselves, and they tend to return to the nest area where they were fed most often.

Well, Johnny would have to fend for himself now, but it looked very much as though he would have the others to show him the ropes.

We went inside and sat on the settee. It was strangely quiet without Johnny running along the back and leaping from chair to chair.

We only lasted half an hour.

"Miserable in here tonight, isn't it?" said Harry.

And we went to bed.

*****

That wasn't quite the end of the story, though. The following day, at dusk, we were tidying up the garden furniture when we heard the sound of young owls chucking in the carob trees which run down the side of the *argaki*. We took a torch to the front gate and leaned on the wall.

The cicadas suddenly started up with their deafening crescendo, and a small owl flew from one of the trees down into a hibiscus bush and back up into the tree again.

I could still hear owlets chucking and I called softly to Johnny. Immediately and unbelievably he flew out of the trees and perched on a branch just above our heads, where he sat bobbing his head from side to side. After a moment or two he abruptly took off and glided down into the garden. I could hear him making the excited noise he made when he saw food coming, and then he flew up on to the electricity wire. I shone the torch on him and we saw he had something in his beak. Johnny was hunting for himself! I directed the light down among the flowers and shrubs and saw there were several cicadas emerging from their underground burrows and starting to climb up the nearest plant stems, trying to get as high as they could before shedding their outer casings and flying away. There were dozens of them. Johnny had more fast food than Mc Donald's. I felt an enormous sense of relief and a great deal of satisfaction. We had actually returned him to the wild where he belonged.

For the next five nights we stood in the same place at dusk and called softly to him. Within seconds he would swoop down and land on the branch above our heads, where he would sit for several minutes. We saw the other two baby owls hunting but they never approached us like Johnny. We could hear the adults calling some distance away, but knew from previous years that once they had moved on after they had finished nesting, we wouldn't be seeing much more of them until the next breeding season began.

The following night when we went out at dusk, we could not hear them chucking and Johnny did not appear when we called. They too had moved on.

Way to go, Johnny.

THEY CALL ME APHRODITE

One November I was given a new name.

When we had been living in the village for more than ten years and were fully committed to the place that had become our home, we were asked to consider the prospect of being baptised into the Greek Orthodox church. We had already decided that we wished to be buried in the tiny *kimitirio* on the outskirts of the village when the time came, so this did seem to be the next logical step. We were at once both touched and honoured that the people should wish to integrate us so completely into their community.

In the event, it seemed to happen suddenly and swiftly. Purely by chance one day, I stopped in a friend's office to photocopy some documents. There, enjoying a cup of coffee, was Kyria Giorgoulla, the lovely lady who was to become my Greek Godmother. She commented on my spoken Greek and the way we had been so warmly accepted as part of the village community, and ended the conversation by saying: "I would like to baptise you, but only if you wish."

A few days later the village priest approached me and said he would be very happy if I took up the offer. Harry, too, would be welcomed into the church if he so desired. He would like to perform the ceremony in the little church of Ayios Minas, which stands by the roadside above the village in the Akamas. Formerly a monastery, this tiny church was built almost eight hundred years ago beside a freshwater spring, and the villagers of Paleo Khorio, the forerunner of our village, used to worship there. Today, services are still held on special occasions, and pilgrims come from all over the island to place candle-wax effigies of the sick below the icon of Ayios Minas who is renowned for his healing powers.

Both of us were very fond of this simple but beautiful build-

The village priest

ing, which has been restored and weatherproofed against the elements. When we passed by on our regular trips into the Akamas, we usually stopped to light one of the small floating candles, and always took our visitors there when we introduced them to the beauty of this wild and rugged peninsula.

The idea took hold and strengthened, and almost before we knew it, Harry had a proposed Greek Godfather - long-time friend and *Mukhtar* of the village, Sotiris.

The Greek Orthodox faith is not as alien as the language makes it appear to foreigners. The *Pistevo* is the Creed we learned in English as children.

I believe in one God...

Only the customs and ceremonies differ from the Church of England, Greek Orthodoxy being more elaborate and stricter in its doctrine and application. There was no conflict in our minds with what we had been brought up to believe. I mused on how many wars would not have been fought and how many lives would not have been lost if we had all been tolerant of the religion of others. We made the decision to go ahead.

*****

I had no idea of the enormous expenses our Godparents would incur. They were obliged to buy each of us a complete set of new clothes from the skin out, for when you dress after the baptism it must be in brand-new, unworn clothing provided by them.

One Saturday my Godmother took me shopping in Paphos. She bought me a beautiful pure wool Chanel-style suit and classic court shoes in soft goatskin to go with it. We then went into a small shop where she chose a few pieces of underwear and asked to be

Longtime friend and mukhtar of the village

shown the latest thing in brassieres.

The elderly assistant, whom I suspect was not a corsetiere by profession, enquired as to my measurements and I duly quoted the Euro size - *ogthonda vita*, 80B. She evidently thought I meant metres, because she delved into a dark cupboard, stacked ceiling-high with cardboard boxes, and produced an awesome garment that was all metal hooks and black satin. At first I thought it was a parachute harness. It was designed to hold back so much flesh it could have been used for bungee-jumping. Fortunately the daughter of the establishment intervened before I became entangled in it, and brought forth something I could recognise as a bra.

Now I had a complete set of new clothing. It only remained for her to buy some fine white cotton fabric which Orania would make into a simple robe, in the classical Greek style, for me to wear during the ceremony.

All they needed to do now was to decide on the Greek name I would be given. It would be either that of a saint or something from Greek mythology. Some of the older men in the village, being unable to come to terms with the foreign sound of Sheila, already referred to me as Aphrodite, and it was unanimously decided that this would be a good choice. The legendary Goddess is closely associated with this area, and several women and girls here bear her name.

I was really quite flattered. After all, they could have come up with something like Medusa or one of the other Gorgons.

Meanwhile Harry, having been kitted out in his new clothes, was to be given the name Charalambos, one of the derivatives of which is Harry, so his Greek name posed no problem. He would not need a robe in the church to protect his modesty - he would wear a swimsuit.

A *swimsuit?* Just how wet were we going to get?

Having been briefed to forego meat in our diet on the

Saturday, we were told to eat nothing at all the next day and to wait until we received a telephone call between ten and eleven o'clock in the morning.

*****

Sunday dawned clear and bright. There was a cool breeze blowing, but it was warm in the autumn sunshine. We sipped our milkless tea and waited, somewhat apprehensively. Things were moving at a very fast pace, with all the arrangements being taken care of by someone else. We felt like a couple of actors waiting for a cue.

The telephone rang, making us jump. It was the summons to the coffee shop. Harry put our bags containing the new clothes into the car and we drove up to the village. My Godmother was waiting, and in the house at the back I was dressed in the long white robe. Over it I put a navy-blue, floor-length caftan to travel up to the church. It was quite a way from the village, so at least there would not be very many people there to see, should we happen to make a mess of things.

It was still and quiet as we got out of the car by the spring, the silence broken only by the sound of birds singing. The priest had not yet arrived to open the door to the main body of the church, but Orania beckoned us into the small annex. This is always left open for pilgrims to come and place their candles and make use of the healing stones, which are said to help promote a cure for various ailments. Here she bade us each light a candle.

Sotiris came with the priest to open up the church, and soon cars began to arrive. *Lots* of cars. Then people, *lots* of people, were bringing in the things required for the ceremony. Several large plastic containers of water, some of it hot, a solid iron tub about a metre long for a font, and all the other accoutrements pertaining to a baptism. Someone rang the big bell outside and the wooden pews began to fill up with villagers. They were delighted for us, and wanted to be a part of the proceedings. Harry's Godfather's family came and gave us tremendous help and support, while I was shepherded along by my Godmother, who had Orania and her daughter, Christalla, to assist her. The priest and *Papatheia* had several of their family members with them, all smiling their delight at the occasion. There were beautiful dark-eyed children all over the place, and the atmosphere could only be described as joyous. I stopped feeling nervous.

Papa Kyriacos came out from the inner sanctum, resplendent in blue and silver robes, his lovely white hair pulled back into the priest's bun. I stood beside Harry at the far end of the nave, looking down the dark interior towards the dozens of flickering candles held by the congregation. They provided the only light, apart from shafts of golden sunlight filtering through a small open doorway, set halfway along one side of the little Byzantine monastery. The ornate silver censer tinkled as it was suspended near the font, and the smell of incense pervaded the air. I was gripped with a sense of unreality. The atmosphere was charged with mystery, and the aromatic smoke, swirling and diffusing the candlelight, made it easy to imagine the cloaked and hooded figures of ancient monks standing silently back in the shadows.

Some of the men half-filled the temporary font with hot water and the priest asked who would baptise us. We stood beside our Godparents while they answered, and we listened intently as each in turn recited the *Pistevo* on our behalf. Then oil was poured into the font and it was blessed. I glanced at Harry standing opposite me and he smiled reassuringly. Neither of us knew exactly what to expect, but we knew these gentle and caring people would lead us through it.

I soon realised I would be taking the plunge first, for several of the women came forward to help remove my outer robe and sandals, leaving me, clad in the classical white gown, to stand alone beside the priest. The stone flags were cold beneath my bare feet and I felt somehow set apart. *Papatheia* smiled encouragingly at me and I relaxed perceptibly.

Papa Kyriacos nodded gently and I stepped into the water. It was actually still pretty hot, and solicitous as ever, he asked if it needed cooling a little. Sotiris caught my eye, and stepping forward, poured in some cold water from one of the containers. I stirred it around with my foot. It was just right.

The priest spoke softly to me in Greek, telling me that when he pressed gently on my shoulders, I was to sink down into the water. I sank, and before I could get up again a veritable deluge of water was poured over my head.

I was assisted from the font and stood while first Papa Kyriacos and then my Godmother anointed me with oil on a piece of cotton wool, each time making the sign of the cross. Then he took a tiny bottle of the sacred *miro,* which is prepared in Constantinople and from there distributed to Greek Orthodox churches all over the world. Only the priest is allowed to administer this precious aromatic oil, and with it he made multiple crosses on my forehead, cheeks, arms, legs, feet and the palms of my hands. I shivered slightly in the soaking-wet robe, and once he had taken a minute pair of silver scissors and snipped my hair three times, I was quickly wrapped in a large towel and taken by the women through to the annex, where many willing hands helped to dry me off and get me into my lovely new clothes.

Dry and warm again, I returned to the main body of the church where fresh water and oil had been prepared for Harry. The

The beautiful old building

141

priest asked the women in the congregation to step outside as he was stripped to his swimsuit. Then, looking tanned and fit, he stepped into the water to go through the same procedure.

When he too had been dressed in his new clothes, I was taken to the font once more where the priest was holding yet another gift from my Godmother - a beautiful gold cross and chain, which he blessed and fastened around my neck. Then came the part that was obviously a favourite with the congregation. My Godmother took my hand, and preceded by the priest, led me three times around the font while everyone sang lustily. Then it was Harry's turn to circle the font, and it only remained for us to take our first Communion in the Greek Orthodox church for the ceremony to be over.

The candles were extinguished and everyone filed out into the warm sunshine. There, beside the beautiful old building with the rugged, pine-clad mountains on one side and the sapphire blue sea on the other, we received kisses and congratulations from everyone while our Godparents passed around the specially wrapped cakes made for occasions like this, and invited people to partake of the delicacies they had brought. There was cake and fruit, nuts and biscuits and whisky for the men. It was a memorable occasion.

Back at the coffee shop, Orania and Christalla laid on a marvellous feast for the immediate participants. There was fresh fish from Latchi and chicken from their own yard. There was salad made in the Cypriot fashion, new succulent potatoes, *tsakistes,* and Orania's red wine. It was sumptuous, and as we ate at one long table, a procession of people came to congratulate us and sit at the other tables while they drank our health in the sweet wine.

It was a day in our lives that we shall cherish and never forget, but there have been other unforgettable moments too. Some we would rather not remember.

THE DAY THE EARTH MOVED

The earthquake struck without warning just after eleven o'clock at night.

All was quiet in the village. It was a cold, dry February night, and as is the custom of people who rise early to work on the land, most of the villagers were in bed and asleep. In our home below the village we were sleeping too, snuggled under a feather quilt against the chill.

Suddenly we woke to noise and confusion. The bed was rocking and shaking, and a deafening and terrifying roar filled our ears. It was as though a hundred pneumatic drills were working a few feet below the bedroom floor. I felt Harry's arms tighten around me and we clung together for what seemed an eternity, but was probably only fifteen seconds or so. The sleeping quarters in our house are downstairs, and upstairs we could hear glass and crockery shattering somewhere. As the turmoil subsided we leapt out of bed and rapidly pulled on tracksuits and sweaters before diving out into the open space beside the swimming-pool. There were sure to be aftershocks, and this may have been only a warning of worse to come.

Outside we could hardly believe our eyes. Such was the force of the tremor that water had gushed up out of the sunken pool and streamed over the patios. Huge terracotta pots had crashed over, their flowers uprooted among the scattered earth and broken shards.

The white walls of the house reflected the moonlight and cast deep shadows on the patio. A superficial check around the outside of the building revealed no obvious signs of major damage, and we thanked God for the seismic frame around which our house is built. Harry disconnected the calor gas system and we sat on a couple of chairs between the house and the studio, holding hands and waiting for the adrenalin surge to subside.

Suddenly the water in the swimming-pool began to move, and a distant rumble became a roar as though an express train was hurtling past directly beneath us. It built to the loud crescendo of the pneumatic drills again and the house moved to and fro before our eyes; it didn't seem possible that it would not collapse. We clung to each other as the ground lifted beneath our feet and the ripples in the pool built up into waves. Again the violence subsided, and we sat there marvelling at and terrified by the awesome fury of the forces nature had unleashed below the surface of the earth.

It was eerie there in the moonlight. There was a strange silence. No night birds called and no tree frogs sang. Even the village dogs were silent. Suddenly, our nerves already frayed, we both leapt as something hit the water with a loud splash and made a low pass over our heads to land in the carob tree behind us. The *niktokorakos* were hungry, earthquake or no earthquake, and they continued to take water and purloin carobs as usual as we sat there.

We wondered how the rest of Cyprus had fared. What was it like in the main towns? The telephone rang, making us jump again. People from the village were ringing to see if we were all right. No one in the community had been injured, but everyone was outside, most of them gathered together in the school playground.

Soon after this the second big aftershock, not as strong as the first, hit us. As the tremor died away, we could hear screams and shouts coming from the village above. Our neighbours Helli and Alfons were away in Austria, so we telephoned our next nearest neighbours at the top of the lane. Kratinos answered.

"We are all OK, but we are staying outside tonight. Come and join us.''

The next call was from Paphos, and we learned that although

the tremor had been felt island-wide, the Paphos district, and in particular our area, had seen the worst of it, the epicentre being in the sea forty miles or so off the Akamas coast. Two people had died in Miliou when the roof of their house had collapsed, burying them as they slept. The nearby village of Pano Arodhes had been devastated, with most of the old stone houses damaged beyond repair. But thankfully there had been no loss of life.

Luckily we still had electricity, so we switched on the television. Cyprus state TV, RIK, was not even on air, but the church channel Logos was broadcasting news as it came in from the outlying villages. If you did not understand Greek you were out of luck, because during the whole episode not one word of information or advice was given out in English, or in any language other than Greek for that matter. Fortunately for us I was able to translate well enough for us to keep up with the news.

The kitchen floor was littered with broken glass and crockery, and a speaker had come off the wall, neatly hitting a pile of dinner plates dead centre before splintering on the floor. We disconnected the electricity, left the mess as it was, and went outside again. We revived ourselves with hot coffee brewed in Harry's art studio, which is a single-storey building and easy to get in and out of quickly.

It was a beautiful night, though chilly, and we walked up the lane to Kratinos' house. There, a crowd of people had gathered under a large open-ended structure with a corrugated tin roof, where Kratinos normally kept his vehicles. The women were wrapped in blankets and everyone was sitting around a small kebab stove, filled with glowing embers, which served to warm cold hands and feet. Kratinos had a wood fire going and kept replenishing the embers as they died out. A radio was broadcasting news of the quake, and one of the younger women was handing round steaming cups of the local coffee. I sat beside Kratinos' mother. She took my hand and rubbed it.

"*Ella, kori,* come near the fire and warm yourself, you are so cold.''

Suddenly there it was, the dreaded distant rumble again. The wooden chairs began to sway beneath us, the pneumatic drills started up, and the tin roof vibrated and rattled noisily. The women repeatedly crossed themselves and called upon the *Panayia* to save them and their children. They were sorely afraid.

There was now a definite lessening of the intensity of the shocks, though, and after we had stayed with them for a while, we became anxious to return to our own home. Everything was peaceful as we walked down the lane in the moonlight, but still no night creatures called. We sat in the doorway of the studio, keeping ourselves occupied with the `Daily Telegraph' crossword and watching the surface of the swimming-pool. The movement of water gave the first clear indication of a further tremor on the way and we could move quickly out and away from the building.

An hour or two before dawn, cold and stiff, we went out to our 4 x 4 pick-up, which was parked under the lightweight wooden carport. We put the front seats into a reclining position and lay back, pulling nylon sleeping bags up over our legs. Sleep would not come, but it was warmer and more comfortable than sitting outside. The moon had set and we looked up through the windscreen into the velvety blackness of a sky spangled with a million bright stars. We felt isolated from the rest of the world, cocooned in a time capsule which swayed gently from time to time as continued aftershocks shook the ground beneath us.

*****

More than two hundred aftershocks were recorded after the

initial earthquake, gradually becoming weaker as time passed. The Department of Seismology had been unable to get an exact reading, but had estimated that it was about 5.2 on the Richter scale. Seismologists in Athens and Israel, however, both recorded 6.2 on the same scale for an earthquake in this area at the critical time - 23.05 hours.

Several village churches were damaged, including our own Ayios Minas, and most old stone houses, built before the regulations requiring seismic frames came into force, sustained some damage - many of them having to be bulldozed later because they were unsafe.

The following day we were inundated with calls from friends all over the island, as well as many from overseas, who had heard about the Akamas earthquake and wanted to know if we were all right. The President of the Republic came to the worst-hit villages to see the effects of the disaster for himself. He quickly promised aid for the homeless residents of Pano Arodhes, and they were soon provided with sleeping tents in the school playground, where a communal kitchen was also set up. In most other villages in the region there were people who feared being buried alive in the rubble of their houses, like the unfortunate couple in Miliou, and they too were sleeping in tents in open spaces adjacent to their homes.

The shocks rumbled on for more than three weeks. Practically the sole topic of conversation in the area was the earthquake. Was this the big one that might have been expected for Cyprus? If so, we had got off lightly, the main damage being in this sparsely-populated area with no high-rise buildings. We still lived on our nerves. The distant rumble of an aircraft approaching stopped all conversation and TV programmes were turned down as we made sure that's what it was. A detonation when they blasted rock in the nearby quarry would have us leaping to our feet ready for a quick exit from the building.

There are lots of do's and don't's in case of an earthquake, most of them easier said than done.

Don't panic. Ok we were frightened, but we didn't panic.

Don't rush out of the building during the tremor. Get in under the door lintel or something like a stout table. Well, ten to fifteen seconds doesn't really give you time to rush anywhere. There is never any warning, and by the time you have woken and realisation has dawned, time is up. In any case our dining table is upstairs.

We were very careful when it came to the bit about gas, electricity and naked flames, but my brain went into neutral when, right after the earthquake, Harry shouted to me.

"Grab whatever you need that's essential! I'll get the briefcase.''

My handbag containing money, passports etc., was on a chair in the bedroom anyway, so I grabbed that, trying desperately to think what else it was I could not possibly do without. Minutes later, out on the patio, the expression on Harry's face would have been worth recording as he saw me sitting there in the darkness holding my binoculars and wearing my brand new designer sunglasses.

Roughly one month later, on Tuesday 21st March at a quarter past eight in the morning, an earthquake of the same intensity as the first hit us, the epicentre being in exactly the same place in the sea. We were upstairs having our breakfast toast and coffee, and hearing the rumble coming and feeling the chairs beginning to sway, we were down the stairs and out by the pool in a time any Olympic sprinter would have been proud of. This time, however, the disturbance was deeper under the earth's surface and the damage was less severe.

We have long since stopped jumping at every unusual sound, but are more prepared than ever we were before. I couldn't help thinking about Marilyn Monroe's unequivocal reply when she was once asked by an interviewer what she wore in bed.

"Chanel Number 5," she breathed huskily.

It may have worked for her, but believe me, a gold necklet and a splash of Opium by Yves St Laurent doesn't do much to cover your confusion when the place is falling down around your ears. I could have done with the thick flannel nightie my Grannie always said I should wear. Now we don't take any chances. We always have spare shoes, socks and tracksuits where we can easily find them, and at least one of the doors downstairs remains unshuttered at night - just in case.

AN ASSIGNATION WITH A PRIEST

The year had been going well up until the time the earth moved. My first book was due to be published within a few months, Harry was enjoying the freedom of painting and sculpting whatever he wished, having completed all the illustrations for the book, and I was enjoying seeing clearly again after having had surgery in November and January to remove cataracts and implant contact lenses in both eyes. The ongoing problem of deteriorating retinas hangs like the sword of Damocles over my head, but the situation is closely monitored by an excellent ophthalmologist, who zaps me with a laser when necessary and who has, so far, managed to ward off disaster.

Spring burst into flower and fragrance all around us. The sun's trajectory was higher in the sky, and we were looking forward to enjoying our first swimming sessions as the water in the pool warmed up.

Nightingales on migration were gathering in the dense shrubbery around the *argaki* and coming into the garden to drink from the birdbaths. These lovely birds are known in Greek as *aedonia* and take their name from a former queen of Thebes, Aedon. At daybreak one morning, when I woke, a single nightingale began to sing. The purity of the notes was heart-stopping, and the poignant flowing melody was like a lament. How easy to believe that Aedon was weeping for her dead child.

Aedon was the wife of Zethus, King of Thebes, and bore him two children; however the King's brother, Amphion, and his wife, Niobe, had seven handsome sons and seven beautiful daughters. Beside herself with jealousy, Aedon devised a plan to kill their firstborn child; but all the children slept together in

150

On his head was a soft pillbox hat

151

one bedroom and, in the darkness, she mistakenly killed her
own son. Zeus changed her into a nightingale and it is said her
deep mourning can be heard in its song.

We were soon up and dressed, for Harry was taking advantage of the good weather and lovely light to photograph and sketch the local people, and loading the camera equipment into the car, we set off on yet another of our expeditions.

*****

In the early morning sunshine the still-sleepy mountains rose mistily up into a sky of faded blue, as we made our way down through Latchi and out on to the narrow road that would lead us to an unspoilt village and an assignation with a priest.

That day it seemed as though the whole world was coloured yellow. The hedgerows were lush and green, and mimosa, bursting into flower, drooped its sunny sprays of blossom in glorious inflorescences down towards the ground. Underfoot, the lemon flowers of cape sorrel nodded on slender stalks, while the rounded yellow blooms of wild mustard swayed in massed array above them. Tall stems of giant fennel spread their pale gold umbels over myriad primrose-coloured ranunculus which carpeted the hillsides, and the bright orange-gold faces of tiny marigolds greeted the sun with a blaze of spectacular colour. Whole meadows shone with the brilliant yellow of crown daisies which bloomed in dazzling profusion, and the lustrous heavily-scented flowers of wild broom splashed the landscape with vivid patches of gold. Even the citrus groves were yellow-hued as ripe lemons on the densely-laden trees glowed brightly in the warmth of the sun.

The priest was waiting at the door of his house when we

arrived. He was dressed for working in the fields, and wore sailcloth trousers tucked into stout boots, and a hand-knitted sweater over a thick shirt. On his head was a soft pillbox hat, made of faded velvet, such as priests sometimes wear when they are not sporting the more formal and familiar stove-pipe hat. He was a picturesque sight with his white beard and twinkling eyes.

He greeted us warmly, later insisting on going inside to change into his blue robe and don the stove-pipe headgear - highly pleased at the thought of being photographed in that. His small, long-haired dog sniffed around our feet and I asked its name.

"*Antigone,*" he replied, and to impress us with his linguistic skills added in English: "Very good boy."

He told us his wife had died, and that without her life was not easy. "Men do not know how to cook and do all the things around the house," he said.

Priests, particularly those in remote villages, are paid a very small stipend and rely on their fields and orchards to provide them with an income. Hens, pigeons, rabbits and goats contribute eggs, meat, milk and cheese to the household, but their care is usually the lot of the women. Much of the priest's time is taken up with services - long and numerous in the Orthodox church - as well as weddings, baptisms and funerals. The priest's wife, or *Papatheia*, plays an active role in the church and her loss could only have increased his workload. I felt a flood of compassion for this hard-working man who spoke so lovingly of his late wife, and I did not envy him the loneliness I knew he must feel at times.

"*Aphrodite, ella mesa.*"

Athinoulla, his neighbour, was calling me. I walked across the huge area behind the house, where a hunting dog was tied on a running lead and a small fluffy house-dog sat on a cane chair - both giving me a noisy welcome. A beautifully marked cockerel shepherded his hens in one place while a huge black sow rolled in the mud grunting, as several small black piglets ran hither and thither. There were rabbits in cages and pigeons in a home-made loft. There were goats and sheep, waiting to go out to pasture, and farm cats washing themselves in the sunshine.

"Ella, kori, pou eess-eh?"

The voice came from a half-open door at the side of the house. I went over and peered into the darkened interior. Athinoulla was sitting on a small stool in front of a large copper *hartchi* under which a low flame burned. She was just adding more fresh goats' milk to the contents and continued to stir it with a tiny bunch of stiff twigs attached to a bamboo stick, before immersing one of the little *talaria* which contained the soft cheese she was making. Other *talaria* full of *anari* stood on the table next to a small tub of erepsin - an enzyme which causes the milk to clot. She reversed the cylinders of cheese in each of the little containers in turn, pressing down with her knuckles to further compress the cheese. Once set, the *anari*, now bearing the marks of the small reed baskets, were removed and placed on a piece of clean muslin in a gauze-covered box attached to the wall, where they could continue to cool, away from the attention of cats and flies.

She brought me up to date with family news and Harry came to sketch her as she worked. When the cheeses were ready and we had been offered refreshment, she prepared to take the sheep and goats to their grazing. We walked a little way with her to the tiny *kimitirio* which she visited every day. Her daughter, a young woman with small children, had died tragically a few years ago and lay in the tiny burial ground next to the ruin of an archaic church.

Athinoulla looked at me and shrugged her shoulders in the

The lovely gnarled and twisted trunk

stoical way of the Cypriot.

"I come here every day and say *kalimera, kori mou.*"

She shrugged her shoulders helplessly again, and we left her to her memories while we drove further up the mountain to find an olive tree.

*****

In the heart of the old village of Pano Arkoudhalia, next to the ancient Byzantine church of Panayia Chryssoleousa, there is a very old olive tree, beside which still stands the heavy stone mill used to extract the oil. The lovely gnarled and twisted trunk of the tree is crowned with wide-spread branches of silvery-green leaves, and this shaded place has an air of peace and tranquillity.

While Harry sketched and took photographs, one of the older residents came out of his small house for the customary welcome and exchange of information. He was pleased to learn that we came from Neo Khorio and immediately listed all the relatives he had there to whom greetings must be given. He then apologised for not inviting us in to his home to drink coffee. His wife was very ill - bedridden with a respiratory ailment - but what could one do? And he too shrugged with that marvellous Cypriot stoicism which seems to sustain them through all manner of hardship.

We stayed to talk with him awhile, then left him, a somewhat forlorn figure, standing in the warm sunshine and drove back down the mountain, through the green and golden landscape, counting our blessings.

AN INCREDIBLE RELATIONSHIP

A few weeks later some friends turned up on the doorstep carrying a large cardboard box.

"Hope you don't mind," they said, "but we don't know what else to do with it."

They followed us upstairs to the living-room, where I put the box on the verandah table and opened the top to find myself looking at a beautiful young kestrel. It was fully fledged but had no hope of flying, for one of its wings was set back at an awkward angle, obviously having been broken at some point, while the other wing drooped down to rest on the bottom of the box. The bird was thin and in poor condition, and tied around one leg was a frayed piece of string. It stared steadily at me from the depths of the box, desperately in need of help, and I was hooked.

Our friends told us of a chance meeting with an English family who had rented a villa in the area. One morning, when the holiday-makers went out on to the patio for breakfast, they found the bird standing dejectedly beside a plant pot in a corner. It quickly swallowed a piece of salami thrown by one of the children, so they gave it more scraps of food and set down a dish of water. When they returned from the beach later that day, it was still there and again accepted small pieces of their meal. In the morning it was in the same place. There it remained for a further two days, making no attempt to move on. The following day the visitors were due to return to the UK, so when they were introduced to our friends at a taverna that evening they happened to mention the bird's predicament. These friends, in turn, knew we sometimes cared for owls in distress, so here they were on our doorstep.

I spoke softly to the bird and slowly inched my hands forward

157

The badly drooping wing

to take it from the box. It screeched loudly, and in an instant hopped on to my hand, out on to the table and right over the balcony rail down into the garden. I hardly dared look, but although it could not fly, it weighed very little and somehow managed to parachute down and land on the rock face, where it stood with the badly-drooping wing making it appear strangely lop-sided.

Oh well, back to the freezer to dig out some of Johnny's chicken liver to defrost. Meanwhile I gave it a dish of water and it drank more than I have ever seen a bird drink in one session. Hardly surprising, I suppose, in view of the fact it had been fed on highly salted cured meats like salami.

I selected a small saucer which I would keep as a feeding dish, knowing the bird would quickly come to recognise it. I took several strips of slightly warm, raw chicken liver and went down to sit on the rock face a few metres away from the kestrel. It looked at me and screeched. I threw a piece of liver on to the rock and it stepped forward and gulped it down. I threw another piece a little nearer to where I was sitting, and it ran to pick it up with the tip of its beak. I lured it a bit nearer with the third piece, and by the time I was down to the last morsel, the bird came to take it directly from the saucer.

I made no attempt to touch it but spoke softly all the time. It was still on the rocks when I went upstairs, but after a while, it hopped and ran to the top of the rock face where there was some shade from the overhanging bushes. It was well-camouflaged, but I was concerned about its vulnerability to stray cats. However, looking at the long yellow legs and feet ending in black curved talons, I began to think that any cat foolish enough to take it on might very well get the worst of the encounter.

I looked out just before dusk and it had gone. My heart sank somewhat and then I saw the bush moving. The bird, unable to fly to roost, was pulling itself up through the foliage using its beak and claws. When it reached the highest point possible it drew one leg up in under itself and went to sleep.

The following morning it was on the rock face again, and when I approached with the saucer of food, it ran towards me and fed straight from the dish. The resident kestrels in the valley hunted three times a day; early in the morning, at noon, and just before dusk. So I decided to feed it at these times, offering roughly the amount of a small bird or mouse each time. I varied its diet with shrews that had fallen into the swimming-pool, small lizards which Harry managed to catch, and the raw necks, hearts and kidneys of chickens. If I had none of this fresh food on occasion, it would eat defrosted chicken liver to which dogs' hair had been added for casting.

It was rather time-consuming having to go up and down to the rock face just to feed it, and I also wanted to start it off on the road to self-sufficiency. So Harry fetched a long wooden plank, resting one end on the rocks and the other on the edge of the upstairs verandah. I took the next meal outside and stood by the top of the plank holding the now familiar saucer. It ran down over the rocks and up the plank like Road Runner and fed eagerly. I left the saucer on the verandah and got on with some work. When I returned we had our first major breakthrough. The bird was sitting on the plank preening itself! This was a sure sign that it was feeling better and stronger. That night it roosted at the top of the plank, and in the morning there was another important development. On the ground below the plank I found its first pellet.

To be in good health birds of prey need to cast pellets containing the undigested fur, bones, claws etc, normally contained in their diet. This pellet was a good indication that its digestive system was returning to normal, and I began to feel optimistic about its future.

It quickly settled into the routine that had been forced upon it; running up the plank to be fed and staying there until the sun got too hot, when it would nip down the plank and get in under the shade of the bushes. It continued to grow stronger. The ligaments of the drooping wing slowly healed and it fell back into place. The diet we provided was obviously suitable, for it continued to cast pellets and preen its plumage which began to take on a healthy sheen.

It was a warm tawny-brown colour, with lovely black bars and striations. The legs and feet were bright yellow, and the black talons were sharply curved and pointed. Yellow too was the cere around the marvellous eyes and the cruelly hooked beak beneath was black and polished, ending in a sharp tip. It was quite beautiful.

I looked at this proud fierce predator and decided to give it a name. Still in its juvenile plumage, I could not tell whether it was male or female, but juveniles closely resemble the female so a woman's name it would be. Falcons are superlative fliers and hunters; I would think of a name for a huntress. Where better to find one than in Greek Mythology?

Atalanta was a huntress. Her father, who had wanted a son, had exposed her on a mountain when she was a baby and left her to die; but she was suckled by a she-bear and grew up with for-midable hunting skills. When her father eventually learned that she had not perished but had grown up into a beautiful young woman, he wanted to marry her off to an eligible suitor. She, however, valued her freedom and her virginity. She killed two centaurs who tried to rape her and devised a test for all those who sought her hand in marriage. She challenged them to race against her. If they won she would marry them, if they lost she would kill them. She was extremely fleet of foot and could run faster than any mortal, and many young men died at the hand they had asked for. At last, from Arcadia, came Hippomenes

161

and so in love was he that he prayed to the Goddess Aphrodite for help. She gave him three golden apples and instructed him to drop them one by one as he ran. Atalanta was so enchanted with their beauty that she stopped to pick them up and Hippomenes won the race.

Thus my falcon became Atalanta. But would she ever fly and become a true huntress like her namesake?

The next stage of recovery was when she began to exercise her wings on the plank where she had plenty of room to really stretch them. A month or so later she began to take off from half-way up. It was rather more gliding than flying, but she was definitely making an effort to get airborne. Not too long afterwards she actually flew a level flight from the studio steps across the swimming-pool to the plank - a distance of some ten metres. I watched with my heart in my mouth in case she dropped into the water, but she made it with ease. Then we had a terrible set-back. A near disaster in fact.

*****

Full of confidence one lunchtime, Atalanta ran and fluttered up the outside staircase of the studio and pattered around on the flat roof. From there she stood looking at the carob trees which line the *argaki* and then, suddenly, launched herself from the roof to land in the nearest tree.

The problem was that the trees were outside the fenced-in area of the garden, and while she could move freely about in them, if she were to flutter down to the ground she would not be able to get back inside again; her wings were not yet strong enough to lift her up from a standing start. She needed a perch of sufficient height from which to take off.

Having just been fed she was having a great time playing about in the trees and ignoring all my efforts to entice her back on to the roof. There was nothing for it but to leave her to get on with it. She'd be down soon enough when she got hungry - or so I thought.

At feeding time I took the saucer of food out on to the verandah, but for the first time she did not come. We searched and called to no avail, and when darkness fell we feared the worst.

I did not sleep well that night, and in the morning it was awful not to see her sitting at the top of the plank preening herself in the early sunshine. We spent most of the day scouring the area around the house without success. When there was no sign of her at dusk we were really downcast. We knew she could neither fly nor hunt for food by herself. Day three came and went, and we had virtually given up hope. It would be a miracle if she had survived as long as this.

On day four the miracle happened. Late in the afternoon I was preparing vegetables at the kitchen sink when I heard a kestrel screeching. I was instantly certain it was ours - I had heard that cry so often. Harry was sceptical.

"Be reasonable," he said. "She's been gone for four days, how can she possibly be alive?"

I looked at him.

"Oh all right. Where do you think it came from?" he asked.

I indicated the direction, and shaking his head, he trudged off down the dirt track, up across a wide field and out of sight. I peeled another potato and jumped as I heard him shout.

"She's here! Quick, come on over - you're never going to believe this."

I tore down the stairs, along the track and through the field.

It was much further away from the house than we believed she could have reached, but when I got there, Harry was standing near a huge carob tree and on the ground beneath the tree was the kestrel.

"She won't come to me," said Harry, "and I'm afraid I'll frighten her away if I try to catch her."

I walked up to the bird, and bending down, held out my arm. Without hesitation she stepped up on to my wrist. Holding her close in front of me, I carried her all the way back to the house.

I put her down on the rock face near the wide, shallow tray of water she had always used for drinking and bathing. She stood in the water and drank and drank. I could see that she had deteriorated badly. She was painfully thin, with lank-looking feathers and the wing that had healed so well now drooped down again to touch the floor.

She was obviously ravenously hungry. She even ate a fallen hibiscus flower while I was warming up some chicken liver. She gulped the meat down easily and quickly, then, with dusk falling, she walked slowly up the plank and settled down to roost. Before I went to bed I went out to reassure myself she was still there. She fluffed her feathers up and looked at me before dozing off again.

In the morning I sat on the floor and watched her while she ate. When she had finished she cleaned and sharpened her beak and claws on the rough wood of the plank as usual, then jumped on to my arm and began to preen herself.

So began a close and incredible relationship between us.

*****

From then on whenever I fed her she always made contact with me; wanting to sit for a while on my arm or shoulder or, more

We set up a board as a feeding table

often, on my head where she would run her beak gently through my hair. I must have been in the running for the title 'the most frequently washed head of hair in the world'.

Gradually her strength returned, and with it the attempts at flying. Now the resident kestrels wheeled overhead screaming their outrage at her and swooping down to attack her on the plank. Atalanta showed no fear of them, rather she shrieked her defiance and stayed put. This was *her* territory, and it was not to be too long before they found this out for themselves.

Doing more running around than flying, Lanta had developed very strong legs and was amazingly dexterous with her talons. I noticed that she spent a lot of time down on the smooth rock face, playing with the small circular pine cones that had fallen from the cypress trees. She liked to pick them up one at a time in her beak and pile them all together. If one rolled away she would be after it in a flash and put it back with the others. I took a cone and threw it towards her and, like lightning, she shot out a talon and grabbed it. No matter how many I threw, how fast I threw them, or how much to one side, she never missed.

Her drooping wing quickly healed again, and her neck became strong from pulling at the tough lizards and bony chicken necks in her diet. Her eyes were clear and the cere around them a lovely bright yellow. Her flying prowess improved day by day, and then suddenly she could fly up on to the verandah from the rock face below. She no longer had need of the plank! We removed it and set up a board, as a feeding-table, on top of the balcony rails across one corner of the front verandah.

I always kept in mind the fact that this was a wild bird, which hopefully would adapt to its new situation and not become a kind of household pet. She took to roosting at night in the cypress trees opposite the verandah, and covered longer distances on each sortie

166

she flew during the day. This, of course, was not to the liking of the resident kestrels who were used to knocking off the odd sparrow from our garden. Two against one, they attacked her with determination. The noise the three of them made while battling it out was incredible, and I had to get used to Lanta streaking on to the verandah to take cover, hotly pursued by two more screeching falcons.

Then we were faced with another dilemma. I noticed the downy feathers under the wing coverts were turning grey, as were the cheeks against which two black stripes were beginning to show. Atalanta, my beautiful huntress, had adult plumage coming in - and was most definitely a male!

*****

In view of his aggressive behaviour towards the other kestrels I did consider renaming him Attila the Hun, but having shortened Atalanta to Lanta (which didn't sound particularly male or female), we decided to leave it at that so as not to confuse him - or us.

There is a false ceiling of trellis, through which bougainvillaea and stephanotis are trailed, above the feeding-table, and in the space above that is the owl box where the Scops owls nest every year. They were not in residence, and Lanta took to spending a lot of time inspecting the box and sitting on top of it to preen himself. One night at dusk, instead of flying over to his usual cypress tree, he settled himself up there to roost.

Before I went inside I cautioned him that it might not be such a good idea. The Johnnies were unlikely to take kindly to a whopping great predator sitting atop the box where they reared their young. The whopping great predator looked down his beak at me,

167

blinked, and ruffled up his feathers. I went in to set the table for dinner.

Halfway through the meal there was a sudden and loud commotion out on the verandah. It came, of course, from the owl box. We slid open the patio doors and shone a torch up into the darkness. Lanta had gone.

I was worried, for although he was bigger and fiercer than the Scops owls, they were predators too and they were wide awake after dark when kestrels were immobile and sleeping. This gave them a distinct advantage over Lanta, who could probably have made mincemeat of them during the day.

It showed us that the Scops owls, whom we normally never see once they have reared their young until they began visiting again in February, kept tabs on their box when it was empty - and were not about to let anyone else move in.

In the morning, when I went out on to the verandah, Lanta flew down to land on my arm. He appeared to be none the worse for being chased away in the dark and ate a hearty breakfast. He never went near the box again, though, even during daylight hours.

He took to flying ever widening circuits around the garden and surrounding fields, and emerged victorious from the war with the other two kestrels. They moved out and he established a sizeable territory with our house as the centre of his kingdom. I sometimes felt sad when I saw other falcons soaring and side-slipping through the sky. Lanta's efforts were very clumsy by comparison, and he could not master the technique of hovering because of his once-damaged wing. Considering what had gone before, however, he had done remarkably well. He was in good health and he was free to come and go as he wished.

If he wanted me he would fly on to the verandah and perch

on the back of a chair just outside the window where I was working on a computer. If the patio doors were open he'd fly in and perch on my chair - or me. If I happened to be in the kitchen he'd appear on the window-sill and walk up and down until I let him in. He always seemed to know precisely where to find me. When I greeted him he would answer back with a staccato chirrup.

When I wanted him I had only to open the window, or go out on to the balcony and call, for him to come swooping in. It always amazed visitors, particularly those who were here on bird-watching holidays, when a brief whistle would bring a wild falcon flying in to land on my arm. Not for Lanta and me the sissy stuff of leather gauntlets and the like. He did not trust anything unusual, and despite those formidable curved talons which easily pierced through the tough skin of a lizard, he would alight on me with the gentlest touch and never once did he scratch me or draw blood.

Not being able to spend as much time in the air as kestrels normally do, he would come in to the feeding table, between meals, bringing some of the little round pine cones so that I would play with him. They kept rolling off and dropping over the edge of the balcony, so we wired a tiny wicker basket to the balcony rail alongside the board. It became a kind of one-sided basketball pitch. It became a very one-sided game too, for although he adroitly caught all the cones I threw and dropped them into the basket, if I scored a goal by getting one directly in while he wasn't looking, he'd immediately pick mine out of the basket with the tip of his beak and drop it over the edge of the verandah. This bird was a sore loser. Sometimes he would roll one towards me along the board, but I didn't dare pick it up for he watched me closely and, at the first sign of a move on my part, he'd rush to grab it in his talon. Although this was socialising and play for him, I felt it was also a good exercise in quickness and co-ordination.

He did not like getting wet, and whenever it rained he would come on to the covered verandah. Harry fixed a wide, hanging perch below the trellis and he would stay there, happily looking down over the valley and the open spaces to the mountains beyond. As soon as the rain stopped he'd be off about his daily business. We weren't sure what that was, considering we were supplying all the food for which he would normally hunt. Actually, he did once catch a small soft-bodied lizard and proudly brought it back, still alive, to the feeding table. He obviously wasn't hungry, and once I had duly admired it he quickly killed it and stuffed it into the little basket to eat later on. He often saved food like this when he had more than he needed. Sometimes he would fly down near the rock face and hide his surplus food under a stone, raking dried grass over it to conceal the site. The only other thing he managed to catch and bring back was one of the huge, pale green caterpillars, with strangely opaque turquoise eyes, which spend their time steadily chomping through the leaves of our oleander bushes until metamorphosing into chrysalides and emerging as beautiful delta-winged hawkmoths.

As spring approached again, although he still came regularly to be fed, he started to spend longer periods away from the house. Then he began to take food with him when he left. He would make a fairly laborious circuit over the valley, which would gain him a considerable amount of height, and then fly off in the direction of the village. A visiting ornithologist, who observed his behaviour for a couple of days, said he was certain he was taking food to a female who was incubating eggs somewhere.

Had he really found himself a mate in the wild? It was tremendous news if he had. Would he eventually bring fledglings back to the feeding-table? The prospect was immensely exciting.

*****

Time passed, and we guessed that he now had extra mouths

170

to feed for he came back more often, hardly stopping to eat anything himself but taking large amounts of food away with him. I was supplying enough chicken liver to feed an army. In the supermarket the lady remarked on our predilection for *sikoti*. When I told her it was for a bird she was horrified.

"But this is expensive," she said. "Give it some bread - birds like bread."

Lanta was getting thin, and more often than not looked to be very tired. There must have been several young ones demanding food, and the too-frequent long flights were taking their toll.

With the spring migration came a team of ornithologists to study birds on the Akamas. They make their base each year at Tavros, a small family-run hotel apartment complex in the village, from where easy access to the surrounding countryside is available for both ornithological and botanical fieldwork. The ornithologists are among those who return there regularly, and we had come to know many of them well. Using Harry's studio as a hide they could get superb shots of difficult to photograph birds like Cetti's warblers which came to the birdbath to drink and bathe. Of course, they were all fascinated by Lanta and there was much speculation as to where the nest might be.

One day two of them called at the house. While one had been checking birds that had been ringed on the Akamas at Ayios Kononas, the other had been walking behind the village with some friends. They came to a big ravine where the sides dropped sharply down for several hundred metres, and set in the vertical rock face was a large hollow. Patiently waiting in the hollow were four beautiful, downy baby kestrels. The thing that interested our visitor most, though, was that perched in a pine tree high above the nest was a kestrel with a damaged wing.

"I'm sure it was yours," she said. "The wing did not fold per-

171

fectly back, just like Lanta's.''

They were leaving the next day, but I knew the area she had described and we made a mental note to visit the site as soon as possible. Then came a quirk of fate which destroyed a unique relationship that might have lasted for years.

Lanta came to the kitchen window and perched on the electricity wire outside. He really did look tired, and I was instantly concerned. Then without warning a bird streaked across the garden and hit him amidships - knocking him off the wire and damaging one of his primary feathers. I could scarcely believe my eyes. It was a woodchat shrike, male and full of pure aggression. I hastily opened the window and Lanta managed to get up to me. He ate some warmed meat and rested awhile. Before long, though, he picked up a chicken kidney and flew off with it in his talon.

The following day he was waiting on the feeding-table early in the morning and soon left with a large chunk of liver. More than an hour later I walked into the kitchen and noticed he was perched on top of Alfons' house opposite. He saw me and took off to glide down towards the window, suddenly veering to the right as the shrike appeared from nowhere and drove at him again. Lanta came at speed in through the open window and landed on me, screeching at the shrike who followed him in and then did an abrupt about turn as it realised I was standing there. I hastily shut the window, not relishing the thought of becoming the battleground with a kestrel perched on me while an angry shrike came streaking in like a ballistic missile.

The woodchat shrikes had nested nearby for some years. We had never located the nest, but saw them regularly at the birdbath, to which they brought their young once they were fully fledged. The male, although quite a bit smaller than Lanta, was fast and aggressive with an extremely stout beak and a cold, staring eye like a shark's. I

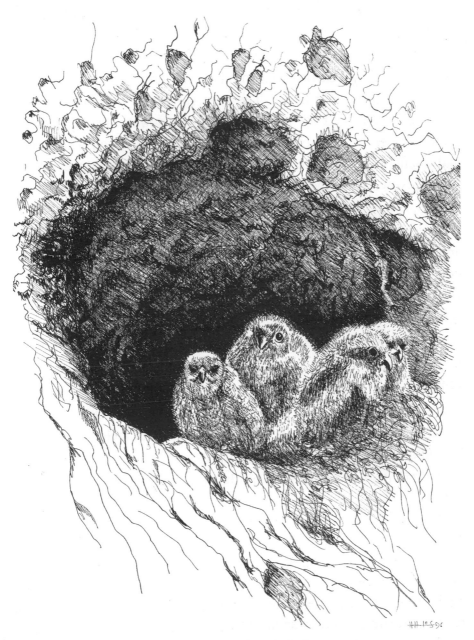

Patiently waiting in the hollow

had often seen it drop down to catch live lizards and then impale them on a thornspike. This rather unpleasant habit has earned the species the nickname of larder birds.

This year the ornithologists had discovered the nest, containing four eggs, in a carob tree some four hundred metres or so away in the field above our house. The next time they checked, the nest had been ransacked by predators; the eggs were broken on the ground beneath, and the nest itself was partly destroyed. The shrikes had abandoned that site and built again very much closer to the house. Now, with the young birds newly-hatched, they saw the kestrel as a serious threat, hence the attacks.

Lanta had neither the time nor the energy to defend himself and his territory. He was over-committed to contributing food to a nest site somewhere else. The shrike, for its part, had decided this was *its* territory, and saw Lanta as an intruder and a predator who was a threat to its young.

It was a no-win situation for my much-loved bird.

The following morning the shrike launched a blistering attack as Lanta came in, striking him in the side with his beak. Another primary feather went askew, and it was all the kestrel could do to get up to the window. He left shortly afterwards, with a chicken heart in his talon, and I never saw him again.

He did not reappear at all that day, and the following morning we set off early for the ravine. The sun was already hot and it was a long walk from where we had to leave the vehicle and proceed on foot. I saw the nest at once. The sun was shining into the hollow and lighting up the pale gold, downy feathers of the two beautiful young kestrels who were perched on the edge of the steep drop, patiently waiting. A further two were sitting close together in the shade at the back of the nest. There was no sign of an adult bird nearby.

We watched for some time while Harry sketched and photographed them. I called to Lanta, hoping in vain that he might be somewhere at hand - perhaps too tired to fly all the way home. But I heard only the raucous cries of the jackdaws who flew over in their slow formation. I felt unutterably sad.

A week later we again visited the nest. Now there were only two young ones. The more adventurous pair had obviously taken the quick way down to the bottom of the ravine. The remaining two looked healthy and were presumably getting wellfed. With that, they began to utter excited cries and reach forward precariously over the edge of the nest. High above a kestrel was wheeling. We remained absolutely still and a female dropped down to land in the hollow, bringing a lizard which the young tore at eagerly. There was no sign of a male bird.

One more visit saw the young ones almost fledged, and the next time we went there the rocky hollow was empty.

I like to think that Lanta's progeny live on as a testament to his courage and fortitude, and I comfort myself with the knowledge that with us he had almost a full year of happy life. He certainly enriched mine.

FIRE!

The weather fluctuated that summer. In July there was an uncharacteristic downpour, and many parts of Cyprus had roads running with water while low-lying districts flooded. Then it began to get hot - very hot. The Eastern Mediterranean is always hot in summer, but this was exceptional. The westerly breeze known as the Zephyr, which normally cools the shores of Chrysochous Bay, did not always blow, and bakingly hot days were followed by stiflingly humid nights. Many of these nights found us cooling off in the swimming pool, looking up at a sky glittering with stars while the moon bathed the surrounding rocks and flowers in its pale light, and night-scented jasmine released its perfume into the warm air.

The shrill noise made by the thousands of cicadas that had hatched was deafening. Each time they stopped abruptly, you could almost hear the silence. Then, as if by some invisible signal, they would all start up again, the sound swelling to an enormous and sustained crescendo. This resonance is actually caused by each insect vibrating its abdomen, but I much prefer to think that Tithonus is still protesting his fate.

Tithonus was a Trojan prince with whom Eos, Goddess of the Dawn, fell in love. The beautiful Eos, who was sister of the Sun and Moon and whose children were the four Winds and the Morning Star, had several lovers, among whom was Tithonus. She loved him for his youth and beauty, and in answer to her plea Zeus granted him immortality. Eos made a fatal mistake, however, she forgot to ask for eternal youth for him as well, and as Tithonus aged over the years, she could no longer bear to look at him and shut him away in a chamber to deaden the

176

Huge rock lizards climbed to drink

sound of his discordant voice. Eventually, as his protests became ever fainter, she changed him into a cicada.

By day the abundance of green trees and shrubs around the house gave welcome shade and relief, as the earth baked under the relentless sun and the burnt umber vegetation became tinder dry, crackling underfoot and releasing dust and spores for next year's growth. With various friends we discussed at length the holes in the ozone layer, and the general consensus was that no one in their right mind could now doubt that global warming was taking place and altering the world's weather systems. Yet despite all the evidence governments were doing too little too late, and still we continued to destroy the delicate balance of the eco-system upon which the very existence of our planet depends.

High winds blew in over the Akamas, but they were hot and dry. Petunias and geraniums wilted in their earthenware pots around the pool and needed daily watering. The shallow stone baths soon became the sole source of water for the neighbourhood birds, and dried up frequently with the heavy demands made upon them. We found ourselves scrubbing and refilling them two or three times a day, but were well-rewarded by the variety of birds flocking to drink and bathe. Huge rock lizards climbed up to drink and then sit motionless, looking as though they had been carved from the very stone itself, waiting for a butterfly or large insect to land in search of moisture from the overspill.

The usual succession of holiday-making friends showed up, getting out of the car after the journey here and plunging into the pool to cool off before flopping into chairs under the sun umbrellas to be handed long, cold drinks. In summer, we live most of the time outside, using the pool-side patios between the bedroom verandah and Harry's studio as an extension of the house. Here we eat and dress informally, our days spent in writing, painting, entertaining family and friends, or simply relaxing on our own when it gets too hot in the afternoons to do anything else but sit in the shade or swim in the pool.

Thus the long hot summer days passed peacefully by until a stranger, driving up our quiet road, considerately left us a cigarette end for which he had no further use.

*****

"Sheila! Get down here and move the car. We have a FIRE!"

It was approaching lunchtime, and I heard Harry's desperate call as I took a pan of sizzling onions from the hob. A gale force wind was blowing, and as the kitchen windows had been removed for the summer, the shutters were wound down to stop the gas from blowing out. So I had seen nothing unusual, nor, because of the onions cooking, had I smelt anything untoward.

I turned off the gas and dashed to the rear balcony, where to my horror I saw thick smoke rising and bright orange flames leaping in the air just outside the garden. I hurtled downstairs and out to the carport where the 4 x 4 pick-up was parked. Flames were licking just a metre away from the vehicle, and Alfons' house was obscured in smoke. I drove rapidly up the lane until I found a safe place, upwind of the fire, where it was wide enough to park without fear of obstructing any fire tenders that might hopefully be arriving.

I ran back down the lane to take over the hosepipe from Harry, directing it to try to stop the spread across the narrow road, while he got the bigger hoses organised to pump water from the swimming-pool. The strong wind was fanning the fire, which hungrily consumed everything in its path. It ran along the dried grass and leapt up into the trees and bushes. Carob trees a few metres away from the actual fire suddenly exploded - bursting into flames and burning like huge torches. It was terrifying.

Helpers began arriving at the double. Alfons and several men, working nearby, were trying to prevent the fire spreading to his house, which fortunately has a concrete wall enclosing the garden. Harry was pumping water from the pool in an attempt to stop it jumping the narrow track to our side of the valley, which has much denser vegetation and lots of trees - not to mention our house.

Men came down from the village and began to beat at the flames, but the fire had taken a firm hold and was out of control. Andreas the Bus came with a shovel attachment on his tractor and dragged firebreaks above the flames to try to stop the rapid run of the fire, but it kept leaping and starting up in other places.

With the somewhat pathetic trickle of water from my hosepipe, I had managed to stop it from consuming a large bush which linked across the track to our orchard. I was helped by the wind, which by the Grace of God had changed that day to blow directly away from our house. Suddenly I saw flames beginning to shoot up in the field on the other side of Alfons' house, threatening a huge carob tree which overhangs the lane and almost reaches some of our pine trees. I rushed down the lane and was valiantly trying to put out this conflagration with the lower garden hosepipe. With the tap full on, this had all the power of a micturating mouse. Then Odysseus, dripping with sweat and blackened with smoke, threw down his beater.

"Saved at last!" he said. "Here comes the fire brigade."

I don't know why it is, but even in the most serious of situations there always seems to be an element of humour. Maybe it's just that my sense of humour is a bit warped, but for me the fire brigade provided a little light relief in the midst of all the chaos, when an over-revving engine heralded the arrival of the tiny bright-red bowser kept to control agricultural fires in the area. It hurtled up the track with great style and dash, spewing chain-smoking firemen in all directions, and promptly parked on my hose-pipe.

There was nothing of the Keystone Cops, though, about the way they set to work to stop the fire from spreading. They quickly assessed the direction of the wind, and while some of the team used water and beaters, others ran with small chain-saws to fell fiercely burning trees. Andreas the Bus dragged more firebreaks ahead of the flames, and where possible pushed earth in over the burning scrub. More and more men from the village came down to help, and as the very strong wind kept whipping up the flames and lifting burning grass in the air to start the fire further along the valley, the Forestry fire-fighting crew arrived with their big tender equipped with power hoses. All local men and all experts in coping with forest fires, they swiftly battled to get the fire under control. A few hours later we were standing, exhausted and smeared with soot and grime, looking at the blackened landscape in which the hollow trunks of carob trees still burned brightly, giving off sparks which glowed red against the darkening sky.

I had been bringing water for the fire-fighters to drink and pour over themselves while they struggled in the intense heat of the fire. Now it was time for a welcome cup of coffee, and we all sat, looking like participants in a minstrel band with our soot-blackened faces, exchanging thoughts on how the fire had started. The Forestry team soon left, but the Agricultural men were to stay for some time, checking the large area that had been destroyed, in case there should be a flare-up. Finally, when the wind had dropped and they had made their last rounds, these exhausted men went home - leaving us to sleep little that night as we got in and out of bed making sure that the smouldering trunks of the carob trees, left to burn out, posed no new threat.

In the morning, looking out of the kitchen windows, it was a sorry sight indeed. The landscape had changed irrevocably. Huge old carob and olive trees that had borne fruit for years had completely disappeared, leaving a clear view through to the roofs of new houses that had previously been masked by their greenery. Now, where evergreen bushes had once provided thick cover for wildlife, only the blackened, twisted stems rose from a barren moonscape of powdery grey ash, while all over hung the acrid smell of burnt vegetation. In the early sunlight it was a scene of utter desolation.

Before long I heard the penny-whistle piping of the male black francolin as he approached his territory. The female has lived nearby for many years, wandering in to the garden and calling for food at will. Somehow, miraculously, she has managed to avoid the hunters - usually by lying low under our lemon tree when they are about. The beautifully marked male was much more of a wanderer, but he frequently came into the garden to feed with the female. His habitual roost was in the thick scrub opposite our lower orchard; but now all the vegetation had been burned away, and only thick ash remained where the previous day there had been dense cover.

I watched as he came to stand on a low stone wall and survey his territory. Another male somewhere down near Latchi called, and he raised his head and answered him. Then, with short staccato cluckings, he walked through the loose ash looking totally bewildered. He went round in circles, lifting his dark red legs high as he went, until finally he stepped up on to a stone and called several times, before flying low across the garden and up into the sloping field behind our house.

*****

Three months later I was getting breakfast ready in the kitchen; it was Sunday and there were hunters around.

182

Notwithstanding the fact that this is a no-go zone for hunting and that shooting is not allowed within one hundred and fifty metres of a house, four or five men were spread out in a line scouring the valley. They were accompanied by several energetic dogs rushing back and forth. A loud explosion made me jump, and looking out of the window I saw a boy, about fourteen years old, holding an unbroken shotgun in one hand while, with the other, he punched the air and did a war dance. Another boy, this one a couple of years younger but also holding an unbroken gun, was sliding down over the bank towards the road, where he dived forward then triumphantly held aloft the beautiful male francolin, one wing still flapping feebly in its death throes.

At my yell of protest regarding their close proximity to us, he hastily stuffed the dying bird into his game bag and clambered back up the bank to join the other boy. One of the hunters, further up the field behind Alfons' house, shouted an instruction at which both boys broke the twelve-bores and moved quickly away from the house.

The minimum age for a gun licence is twenty-one years, and apart from their complete disregard for the law, it is difficult to imagine what goes on in the mind of a parent who would allow boys as young and irresponsible as these to be in possession of such lethal weapons. It was pure luck that one did not kill the other in the mad scramble for the bird, considering that only one barrel had been fired and neither gun had been made safe. And it was lucky for me that I was not out watering the plum trees, for the shot was fired across the orchard from a few metres away, catching the bird, flushed by the pack of dogs, as it rose over the burned ground that provided it with no cover.

I was haunted by the expression of sheer joy on the boy's face when he killed this handsome bird, which is now becoming a rare sight in Cyprus. How sad to take such unmitigated delight in destroying a beautiful creature, one glimpse of which makes most people who come here catch their breath in wonder. Poor tormented francolin. Poor misguided boy.

A LITTLE OF THE UNEXPECTED

Enormous changes have taken place in the area since we first made our home here. Many of the older generation have passed on, and with them much of the old way of life. Developers woo the heirs to the land with vast sums of money, and villas and apartments are springing up in once idyllic tracts of countryside. Others, forced to emigrate because there was no work to be found, are now returning to the family property to set up businesses associated with tourism. Foreigners, mainly those who have retired, are coming here to settle in large numbers - some finding their dreams come true, but others falling by the wayside.

A great many expatriates first fall in love with the island when they come on holiday. Won over by endless golden days and romantic moonlit nights, the idea of leaving their cold, grey mother-country to bask forever in a land of perpetual sunshine, where inexpensive taverna meals and freely flowing wine become the norm, is hard to resist. Add to that the legendary hospitality and friendliness of the local people and too often, without enough forethought, the die is cast.

The happy ones have faced up to the challenge of the immense change from working life to retirement in a completely different environment. They have made new friends and organised their lives the way they want them. Others find integration into a new community difficult, and long for home. They can often be seen sitting aimlessly outside the coffee shops, watching the tourists go by and wondering what they can do with themselves for the rest of the day.

For us the days are all too short, and the time ahead seems always full of things we want to do. Sometimes, when Harry is painting or drawing in the studio and I am at the computer engrossed in writing, the hours flash by with no thought of domestic chores or lunch. Whoever reaches a natural break first will put the kettle on for coffee or whatever, knowing full well that the other needs to finish the drawing or chapter being worked on. All mundane things seem to be forgotten - we will tackle them together later on. Now and then, however, our total absorption results in a little of the unexpected.

*****

One extremely hot day last summer I was proof-reading a pile of manuscript on the shaded downstairs verandah overlooking the bay. I had left open all doors to the house to allow the slight westerly breeze through. Harry was some considerable distance away behind the studio, sitting in the shade of a big old carob tree, absorbed in carving a classical Greek head from a block of sandstone. He was the first to cave in and come in search of a cup of coffee. He walked through the garden, across the patios that surround the pool, and on to the verandah outside the bedroom, calling to me that he was going upstairs to put the kettle on. As he entered the house he stopped.

"What on earth are you doing out there?"

"I'm checking through manuscript."

"What's all that noise, then?"

I came to join him in the hallway between the two bedrooms and heard a flapping, slapping sound. We looked at each other and then at the partly-open bathroom door. Harry reached out and pushed it back and we found ourselves looking at the writhing coils of a two-metre-long black snake as it flailed around trying to get out of the bath.

We shut the door hastily. This was worth a photograph.

"I bet George would like this one for his exhibition," said Harry. "It's a beauty."

I picked up the telephone and dialled.

"There's a snake in my bath, George."

Snake George's interest was instantly aroused.

"What kind is it?"

"*Coluber jugularis,* a beauty."

"How big is it?"

"About two metres."

"I don't want it then, I've got a couple bigger than that. Just pick it up and put it out in the garden."

I replaced the receiver. Thanks a lot, George. Now all I had to do was grab hold of a couple of yards of struggling snake and haul it out into the garden.

By now Harry was taking photographs of the poor creature, which presumably had been seeking somewhere cool and had managed to find enough purchase on the tiles to get into the bath, where it was floundering helplessly, unable to get up over the smooth contours of the porcelain.

"I bet Alfons would like a picture of that," I said. "Let's give him a bit of a surprise."

Alfons is not over fond of snakes. We have a black one called Oscar, grown to almost three metres in length, who lives in the garden and who plagues Alfons and Helli from time to time by sunbathing on their wall and lurking in their flower beds. He mainly keeps himself to himself, though, and apart from reducing the bird and lizard populations a bit, he does no harm. He also polishes off rats and mice which might otherwise destroy the bark of the carob trees. As the years have gone by we have all become quite fond of Oscar, and as long as he doesn't invade their house, he lives in peaceful co-existence with our neighbours.

I looked across the track to see Alfons watering his lavender.

"Alfons, bring your camera, there's a great photograph here."

Alfons, totally used to my interest in wildlife and things unusual, asked no questions. Pausing only to pick up his camera, he came right across.

"Where is it? What is it?"

"It's in the bath."

"In the bath! Ah-ha - it's one of those big black spiders."

Alfons knows I can't stand the big African bird-eating spiders.

"Not exactly, but believe me it will make a good photograph."

By this time we were at the bathroom door and Harry invited Alfons to go in. He opened the door and immediately leapt back a foot.

"*Panayia mou!* It's a snake. Call Snake George."

"I've already tried that. He doesn't want it. We have to get rid of it ourselves. Would you like it for your garden, Alfons?"

My neighbour looked at me askance. He knows my sense of humour only too well. He took some photographs.

The poor snake was getting pretty exhausted with its unsuccessful attempts to scale the bath's interior, and I wanted to set it free as quickly as possible. Knowing it would be more traumatic for it to be handled than helped, I passed Alfons the sweeping brush and asked him to do the honours. He put the brush in the bath and our uninvited guest made immediate use of the makeshift bridge to get its head up over the edge. Alfons then grabbed hold of its tail and lifted it out on to the floor, where it waited a moment before slowly slithering out of the front door and disappearing among the flowers and shrubs.

I am still puzzled as to why it chose to come into the house, for to do so it must have had to pass a whole swimming-pool full of water where it could have more easily had a drink and cooled off. Perhaps it liked the cool, smooth feel of the marble tiles indoors. Fortunately we did not have visitors at the time, for beautiful creature that it undoubtedly is, a two-metre snake in the bathroom when you go to take a shower is likely to put a bit of a dampener on anyone's holiday spirit!

*****

Inevitably, over the years, we have had numerous encounters with Oscar in the garden, and the sudden surprise and instinctive recoil action of the person on the receiving end of his attentions is surpassed only by the mirth of those who witness the event and never intend to let it be forgotten.

Below the front verandah there is a terraced shrub-bed where a beautiful plumbago has grown to exquisite maturity, draping its profusion of sky-blue blooms over the stone walls. Early one warm summer evening I was leaning against the wall, directing water from the hose-pipe into the base of this lovely bush, when the flowers suddenly erupted in front of me and about three thick metres of black snake shot across the hose-pipe and up over my arm before streaking across the garden at an incredible speed. My shriek must have been heard in Latchi, but I got no sympathy from my spouse who was doubled over, almost hysterical with laughter, on the verandah above me.

As they say, though, he who laughs last...

He was still ho-ho-ho-ing about my hair-raising experience and bemoaning the fact that he hadn't had a camera with him at the time, when some weeks later he was kneeling by the corner of the house clearing a drainage pipe that had become blocked with leaves. There was dense foliage around the bottom of the pipe and I called across from where I was sitting by the pool.

"Watch out for snakes."

"No way *I'm* going to get caught," he replied smugly. "I probed in there with a stick before I started."

He finished clearing the plastic bend he had removed and pushed it back on to the down-water pipe before straightening it with a sharp tug, causing Oscar, who was quietly inspecting birds' nests at the top of the bougainvillaea, to lose his grip and come flailing down to land with an almighty `thwack!' on the stone path right beside him. He must have leapt at least two feet off the ground, and I bet *his* yell could have been heard in Turkey - though I doubt they would have found the expression he used in any dictionary.

We have learned to accept such encounters, having built our house in a wild and unpopulated area, and generally find these visitations more fascinating than frightening. We do sometimes tend to forget, though, that people living in town houses in the UK are not as used to the variety of wildlife that we now take for granted.

NO NIGHT TO BE SLEEPING INDOORS

My brother knows Cyprus well, but it was after many years away from the island that he and his wife - an old hockey adversary of mine - returned to stay with us at the Back of Beyond.

One lovely summer night, having swum and sunbathed all day, we were preparing to go down to Latchi to dine on the fresh fish for which the little port is famous. David gazed up at the glittering panoply of stars.

"This is no night to be sleeping indoors," he said to his wife.

She guessed what was coming and quickly knocked the idea on the head.

"Forget it," she replied.

Undaunted, he set up a safari bed on the patio outside their bedroom.

"I often slept outside in the old days," he said. "I'll crash out here when we get back. When do you ever have the opportunity to do this at home? Just look at all those stars."

We went down to Latchi and sat by the lovely little stone-walled harbour to enjoy our dinner and watch the moon rise over the mountains. The haunting strains of a Greek love song floated on the air, just audible above the sound of water slapping against the hulls of fishing boats rocking at their moorings. I drank only soda-water, leaving the other three to enjoy the dry, light white wine served with the meal.

A few merry hours (and people) later, I drove us up the hill. My brother, still waxing poetic about the loveliness of the night, opened the front door and kicked off his sandals before going inside. The other two, giggling about something that was evidently uproar-

The lovely little stone-walled harbour

iously funny, were close behind him. I closed the front gate and turned to see them all shooting out of the front door again, falling over each other in their haste. Just inside the hallway was a scorpion, and my shoe-less brother had narrowly missed treading on it.

Scorpions in Cyprus are not the lethal great black things that inhabit the desert regions, but although smallish and semi-transparent, they can give you a pretty painful jab. The hubbub subsided, and still recovering from the encounter with the *rigolorous,* they began to mount the stairs to the living-room. It was coffee-time.

As I followed them in, I saw something moving on the wall just to one side of the front door and shone a torch to see a beautifully patterned European cat snake, erect and poised, with its head turned towards me. The lovely brown eyes with their deep black centres, which give this slender snake its name, reflected the beam of light from my torch, exactly like a cat's eyes seen at night.

I should have left it at that, but with the full moon high in the sky, I knew I would be able to get some good video shots of the creature against the white wall of the house. I called up to Harry, asking him to bring down the video camera and a spare torch.

Of course they all came tumbling down the stairs together, and there followed a somewhat hilarious ten minutes or so, during which I attempted to film the snake while answering questions coming at me from all directions like machine-gun fire.

My subject posed prettily, moving slowly, and the film turned out well, apart from the bits where my torch-bearers could not seem to keep the beams of light directed at the snake, and I got some puzzling shots of a blank wall. The sound effects were rather unusual too, as my assistants kept laughing at each other's shortcomings and my attempts to shut them up.

"That's the prettiest little snake I've ever seen," said David.

"I think I'll pick it up."

"It's poisonous, you know," volunteered Harry helpfully.

There followed a slight pause as hands were sharply withdrawn.

"Is that true, Sheila?" said my sister-in-law.

"Yes, but it's a back-fanged species and its mouth is so tiny it can't do you any harm."

Despite my reassurance I sensed a further withdrawal, and the torch beams wavered more than ever. A closer inspection of the snake by the intrepid trio now seemed unlikely, so I switched off the camera and watched the small nocturnal snake glide down the wall and disappear under the hibiscus bushes, to carry on hunting for its supper.

A cup of coffee later I went across to the studio, where Harry and I would be sleeping, and passed my brother on the bedroom verandah pulling his safari bed back inside. I expect the moonlight was a bit too bright for him.

*****

The next morning dawned full of rosy light and the promise of another glorious day. We breakfasted on the living-room verandah, listening to the melodic sound of sheep bells as the shepherd drove his flock along the track in search of good grazing. The valley unfolded below us, strewn with trees and shrubs of differing shades of green, and a soft susurration arose as the breeze sighed through golden fields of whiskered barley bordering the sea. The steady throb of diesel engines drifted up from Latchi where the local fishermen were returning from hauling in their nets. The water in the bay shimmered densely blue in the early morning sunlight, and the gaily

A beautifully patterned European cat snake (from a photograph by Hans-Jorg Weidl- Snake George)

coloured boats disturbed its stillness, dragging white lines of foaming wake behind them.

Fishing boats were the objective today. We had planned a trip to the little harbour at Pomos on the other side of the bay, to combine a morning's sightseeing with some photography.

All early risers, we had cleared up and were on our way before seven o'clock. We passed through a slumbering Latchi and the outskirts of Polis Chrysochous before turning on to the road that runs eastward along the coast.

On our left the sea sparkled with the brilliance of a million sapphires as a soft breeze ruffled the surface and the faceted water reflected the bright sunlight. On our right the fertile plain was planted with tomatoes, cucumbers, courgettes, aubergines, melons and bananas, and behind, the terraced foothills rose up into the forested mountains.

The smooth tarmac road led on through Limni, and the small villages of Argaka, Yialyia and Ayia Marina before rising up to Neo Thimata with its tiny church perched on a headland overlooking the sea. Now the road twisted along the top of rugged cliffs rising up from rocky coves below. Jagged grey-black rocks jutted from the sea, and the shallow water around them was a translucent turquoise.

Passing through Pomos we turned left towards the harbour and drove down the steep track to the quayside, where the fishermen and their wives were taking the night's catch from their nets. Today the fish were plentiful; there had been a run of *skoumpri*, a kind of small mackerel, and the woven baskets gleamed silver with fish. Harry photographed one of the fishermen who had a handsome, quintessentially Greek face. He preened his moustache and posed self-consciously. The best shots Harry would get would be, as always, when I engaged the subject in conversation and he forgot

The little harbour at Pomos

about the camera.

David, our expert on fish, said these would be delicious grilled on the barbecue. So we bought some for supper, getting almost twice as many as we had paid for tipped into the cold-bag by the smiling wife of the *psaras.*

Before we left we went to explore a cave further along the shore in which, I had been told, a supply of fresh water could be found. Here the sand was grey and gritty among volcanic-looking rocks. A kingfisher was fishing in the shallows, its brilliant blue plumage gleaming metallic in the sunlight as it streaked across the water. At the back of the narrow beach we spotted a cave, and clambering up to the entrance saw that it was quite small; a few paces would easily take us round the interior. Near the entrance, centrally positioned, was a hole in the ground. Here it was, a natural well providing a source of sweet water just a few metres from the sea. The shepherd, whose flock wandered over the rocky and sparsely vegetated ground above the cave, drew water from this well for his sheep. There was a battered bucket, to which a frayed piece of rope was attached, and wedged between some rocks above the beach was a long metal trough where the animals gathered to drink. This simple system worked as it had for generations, needing no machinery and causing no pollution. The scattered sheep-droppings fertilised the ground and nourished the growing grass and flowers. The picturesque sight of the long-tailed sheep and the familiar sound of their bells was a potent reminder of rural life - before the intensive and expensive farming methods now employed in so many other countries prevailed.

We headed back to Neo Khorio, and that evening as the strangely luminescent twilight bathed us in its glow, we cooked our fish by the pool over red-hot embers of carob wood, and speared pieces of fresh, chilled watermelon on our forks while we sipped a local wine. We watched the light slowly fade and the calm water in the bay darken into a lake of deepest indigo from which plum-coloured mountains rose up into a sky stained with misty shades of violet.

I looked at my much-loved brother and his slender wife, sun-tanned and laughing, with the handsome and talented man who has shared my life; and in that moment I knew the true meaning of contentment.

FRIENDS AND STRANGERS

That autumn we had more strangers than usual.

Early one morning I was washing dishes and looking out over the bay. There had been rain in the night, and the sea was flat calm in gentle shades of blue-grey, while the mountains stood stark and black against a sky washed with pale apricot. Harry was stacking wood behind the studio when he suddenly stopped and shouted to me.

"Come and have a look at this!"

I went downstairs, and there on the wall just above the pile of logs was the biggest African bird-eating spider I had ever seen. I stared at it in horror.

"No good getting the mop," said Harry. "You'd need an Exocet missile to be sure of killing that."

In previous years we had disposed of those that found their way indoors with a damp mop, but this one was truly enormous, and only feet away from the studio door.

Harry fetched a wide-necked paint-jar and a piece of stiff card, and showing courage above and beyond the call of duty, neatly flipped it off the wall into his jar. He took it into the shower room in the studio and up-ended the container on the floor. The spider spread its awful legs out and tested all areas for means of escape. When it found none, it settled balefully on the floor inside its glass prison and waited.

We waited too - for Snake George to show up. He would be delighted to have a live specimen this size for added interest in his new exhibition near Peyia, where he was busy constructing a special site in which the island's reptiles and amphibians could be seen in their natural environment.

That afternoon some strangers came to the gate. Apologising for the intrusion, they said they were staying in the village overnight and had hoped to be able to meet us. We invited them in and the lady asked, somewhat nervously, if Oscar was in the garden. I assured her I had not seen him for a couple of weeks; whereupon she opened her book and pointed to Harry's realistic drawing of the African bird-eating spider.

"Are those spiders *really* as big as all that?" she enquired.

"Funny you should say that," said Harry. "Follow me." And he beckoned them into the studio where he slid open the door to the shower room.

The spider, monstrous enough to have its legs touching all round the sides of the wide jar at once, looked even bigger inside the glass because of its magnifying effect. Our visitors were speechless. Harry bent down and the spider reared its front legs up against the side of the jar, causing the couple to flee the studio with an impressive turn of speed, and I got the feeling they wished they'd never asked.

Within a week Snake George came with his wife and their two little daughters, and as expected, went into raptures over the spider. He confirmed it was a large male, and much to my relief took it with him when he left.

Others came in search of the back of beyond - almost all wanting to see specific things like the owl box, the swimming-pool or Oscar. I had no idea that an account of our simple way of life here would touch such a chord in so many people, but it appears that many of the things which so fascinate us intrigue a lot of other people too. They are mainly insignificant events which go unnoticed every day, but here we are in a unique and privileged position to witness them. Often these moments are shared with others, and the effect on people whose lives are touched by nature in this way is sometimes quite profound.

*****

One spring, notwithstanding Oscar who habitually devours their young, the Spanish sparrows were determined to build their nests again in the bougainvillaea that climbs up over the house. There were more males than females, so competition was fierce - and when a female showed up the noise and posturing of the males increased to manic proportions.

One male, seemingly unable to find a spot he liked on the left where all the others had begun to build, started to weave his nest on the right-hand side of the verandah in a fork of bougainvillaea, just a foot or so away from the owl box. I fervently hoped the owls wouldn't use his sleeping nestlings as a food source for their own when both families hatched. As it was I needn't have worried. The poor little devil didn't get that far.

At noon one day four of us were seated around the big table in the living-room for lunch. I was tossing a green salad and looking towards the front verandah, when I saw the lone little male zoom across from his nest site to the more heavily-populated area where a female had just landed, sending all the unattached males into a frenzy of display.

Suddenly, with no warning of any kind, a sparrowhawk sped in over the balcony and disappeared through the thickly-massed and spiky branches of the bougainvillaea. I was still trying to take in this totally unexpected event when it re-emerged through the foliage with a Spanish sparrow in its talon, and swooped silently down over

A trip to the coffee shop is always a must

the balcony rail and across into the pine trees that line the garden. We looked at each other in amazement: the whole incident had taken only a few seconds.

Sadly, the victim was the poor little male who had braved the side where the owl box is located. How do we know? By the unfinished skeleton of the perfect little nest he had begun to construct, which remains there to this day.

The people who witnessed this little tragedy with us had an interest aroused which surprised them, and they are now confirmed and keen birdwatchers.

Another friend, who stayed with us one February, got out of bed on a moonlit night to investigate a strange noise he heard coming from the patio outside his bedroom. He opened the door and got the fright of his life as Botham swooped in under the arches on his second circuit of the pool. Our rudely-disturbed guest had no idea there were fruit bats here, nor any inkling of their size and the noise made by the flapping of their leathery wings, and he was instantly spellbound.

Botham obliged him with another run, and in the bright moonlight was clearly visible as he dipped into the swimming-pool for a mouthful of water. After that our visitor was hooked. He related the incident to anyone who would listen, and spent the rest of his holiday nights bat-hunting in the small hours. He paid the price, though. No longer addressed by his proper name, he is of course universally referred to as Batman.

Our long-suffering friends are used to the idiosyncrasies of village life and the uniqueness of the wildlife here, and follow events with great interest. They get to meet the local people when they visit, for a trip to the coffee shop is a must, and I love interpreting at these meetings. Always giving strangers a warm welcome, the villagers are healthily curious about our visitors, and very frank and open in their remarks.

Harry has been posted at various times to bases which have a military hospital attached, and many of our friends are consultants who come to see us when they are on detachment in Cyprus. One unassuming orthopaedic specialist returned from the village almost in a trance one day after someone, who the previous year had fallen from a donkey and fractured his pelvis, beckoned him into the back yard. There, amid the donkeys and hens, he dropped his pants for the distinguished visitor to give an opinion on the injured portion of his anatomy.

"I've worked in field hospitals and makeshift theatres before," he said, "but that's the first time I've done a clinic in a donkey-shed with a cup of coffee in my hand."

There are boundless opportunities to witness humour in the situations in which we continually find ourselves, and Harry knows that sooner or later I will probably write about them. I have heard him mutter to himself on more than one occasion: "The things I do to get you another chapter..."

Our friends too, knowing well my sense of humour and love of the ridiculous, are not really surprised by anything that happens here, but now they are getting wise before the event and word has gone round.

"For God's sake don't tell Sheila anything even remotely embarrassing, or you're liable to get booked."

EPILOGUE

Beyond the village and the fields, the mountains of the Akamas dream on, rising silver-misted in the fragrant dawn. Serene and constant in an ever-changing world, they guard the hidden secrets of this timeless land, while far below the warm sea laps on white-gold sand in once deserted coves. But further in, around the azure waters of the bay, the future beckons and the land must pay its way, for Cyprus cannot live on dreams alone. Inevitably change must come.

So progress has begun, and today the pleasing green of newly planted trees delights the eye, and flowering oleanders line the road as Latchi grows into a modern resort. But with it progress brings a wealth of other things. There are cars to park and mouths to feed, and now the wild and sandy beach, where once I stood to watch the herons fly towards the mountains of Akamas, blooms with grass and flowers and sun-beds row on row; and low white buildings, tourist-full, reflect the sun beside imported palm trees.

And more tall palms give graceful shade on pleasant walks around the harbour-side. The creaking wooden pier, where deep-sea fishing boats tied up and strong men strained to bring the gleaming swordfish catch ashore, is going soon; the big fish, swords removed while still at sea, land cleaned and chilled. The sponge-boats too have gone away, and divers do not come to wash their haul and lay the pale gold sponges in the sun to dry.

The age-old rocks of Asprokremma groan beneath the weight of concrete being poured. Weathered stone that stood the test of time and tide and seismic thrust is blasted skywards - raining down, fragmented, on to levelled ground where soon new buildings will burst forth, more and ever more, like rows of warriors sown from dragons' teeth in ancient Colchis.

The lovely, lonely beach will swarm with tourists seeking

dreams of sun and sand. The sea will shimmer just as blue and gently wash the golden shore, while strangers gaze enchanted at the view, and walk through landscaped gardens laid with artistry. But herons will no longer come to stand like statues in the morning mist, and turtles, needing solitude and space, will swim to more deserted shores to make their nests.

The donkeys, too, have almost had their day. Now jeeps in convoy churn the dust of ancient Akamas, and karaoke music blares where Adonis and Aphrodite lay. And more jeeps crowd the tiny church of St. Minas, as flowers are trampled in the field where monks once toiled beneath the sun.

New roads traverse the dreaming poppy-fields that clothe the valley down towards the sea. Bright flowers, uprooted, wilt upon dried earth and rocks exposed. And olive trees, wrenched from the soil, shed silvery leaves like angels' tears.

for man, proud man... plays such fantastic tricks
before high heaven as make the angels weep.

The cobbled village road, where game birds crossed and donkeys carefully picked their way, is concrete now: the hum of summer honey bees lost in the angry hornet-whine of mopeds racing by, and early morning birdsong drowned in builders' noise.

New homes, the size and splendour of the Taj Mahal, stand on slopes where orchids and rock-roses bloomed and chukar wandered, cackling, through; and the high-pitched yelp of man's best friend besets the ears, where once we heard the rolling bark of foxes on the prowl.

So there are those with different dreams, whom progress suits, who think the untamed land a backward thing. But not for me to question others' dreams when mine have been fulfilled.

For I live in a land not yet despoiled amid the despoliation wrought by man upon the natural world. And living here, I know that I am blessed. For I look out on lilac mountains, etched against a sky where falcons soar and lift my spirit up to heights that some can only dream of.

As the fishing port grows into a modern resort

GLOSSARY

acheron	chopped hay
afterburners	flaming liqueur
alepou	fox
anari	local cheese
avrio	tomorrow
avrio, koukla mou	tomorrow, sweetheart
argaki	stream bed
birazi?	does it matter?
canella	cinnamon
echo to klithi	I have the key
ella	come
ella, kori	come, daughter/girl
ella, na ba-meh	come, let's go
ella na theis	come and see
fugaro	chimney
glyko	traditional Cypriot sweet
halloumi	local cheese
hartchi	large cauldron
kala Christouyenna	Happy Christmas
kalimera kori mou	good morning, my daughter/girl
kalikantzari	mythological dwarf-like creatures
kapnistiri	incense burner
kastana	chestnuts
kefalotiri	local cheese
kopiaste	come and share our meal
kimitirio	burial ground
Kyrie eleison	God have mercy
lagos	hare
laspi	labourer
loukanika	sausages

lounza	smoked pork loin
manitaria	mushrooms
mastros	foreman
mespila	loquats
miro	precious oil
moufflon	wild sheep
mukhtar	headman of village
na ba-meh?	shall we go?
na su zisi	you are to be congratulated (May he/she live for you)
niktokorakos	fruit bat
o theos een-eh megalos	God is great
oke	old weight measure
orfos	grouper fish
ochi	no
Panayia mou!	Holy Mother of God!
papatheia	wife of a priest
pervolia	orchards
pilo	mortar
pistevo	I believe
pou eess-eh?	where are you?
psaras	fisherman
rigolorous	scorpion
serpentina	configuration of copper pipes
sikoti	liver
talaria	small reed basket
then birazi	it doesn't matter
tsakistes	cracked green olives
xeni	strangers
chronia polla	long may you live
yassoo	hello
zivania	alcohol distilled from grapes